INHERIT
THE WIND

INHERIT THE WIND

Jerome Lawrence and Robert E. Lee

"He that troubleth his own house
Shall inherit the wind."
PROVERBS 11:29

BALLANTINE BOOKS • NEW YORK

A Ballantine Book
Published by The Random House Publishing Group

Published in the United States by Ballantine Books, an imprint of The Random House Publishing Group, a division of Random House, Inc., New York, and simultaneously in Canada by Random House of Canada Limited, Toronto.

www.ballantinebooks.com

ISBN 0-345-46627-6

Manufactured in the United States of America

This edition published by arrangement with Bantam Books, a division of Random House, Inc.

First Random House Edition: September 1955
First Bantam Books Edition: October 1960
First Ballantine Books Edition: November 2003

OPM 9 8 7 6 5 4

INHERIT THE WIND was presented by Herman Shumlin, in association with Margo Jones, at the National Theatre, New York City, April 21, 1955, with the following cast:

(IN ORDER OF APPEARANCE)

MELINDA	Mary Kevin Kelly
HOWARD	Eric Berne
RACHEL BROWN	Bethel Leslie
MEEKER	Robert P. Lieb
BERTRAM CATES	Karl Light
MR. GOODFELLOW	Salem Ludwig
MRS. KREBS	Sara Floyd
REV. JEREMIAH BROWN	Staats Cotsworth
CORKIN	Fred Herrick
BOLLINGER	Donald Elson
PLATT	Fred Miller
MR. BANNISTER	Charles Thompson
MRS. LOOMIS	Rita Newton
HOT DOG MAN	Howard Caine
MRS. MCCLAIN	Margherita Sargent
MRS. BLAIR	Ruth Newton
ELIJAH	Charles Brin
E. K. HORNBECK	Tony Randall
HURDY GURDY MAN	Harry Shaw
TIMMY	Jack Banning
MAYOR	James Maloney
MATTHEW HARRISON BRADY	Ed Begley
MRS. BRADY	Muriel Kirkland
TOM DAVENPORT	William Darrid
HENRY DRUMMOND	Paul Muni
JUDGE	Louis Hector
DUNLAP	Fred Miller
SILLERS	Fred Herrick
REUTER'S MAN	Edmund Williams
HARRY Y. ESTERBROOK	Perry Fiske

Townspeople, hawkers, reporters, jurors, spectators, played by: Lou Adelman, Joseph Brownstone, Clifford Carpenter, Michael Constantine, Michael Del Medico, James Greene, Ruth Hope, Sally Jessup, Julie Knox, Patricia Larson, Michael Lewin, Evelyn Mando, Sarah Meade, Gian Pace, Richard Poston, Jack Riano, Gordon Russell, Carroll Saint, Robert Shannon, Maurice Shrog.

Directed by Herman Shumlin

Settings by Peter Larkin

Lighting by Feder

Costumes by Ruth Morley

Assistant Director: Terese Hayden

INHERIT THE WIND was first presented at the Dallas Theatre '55 on January 10, 1955. The cast included Edward Cullen, J. Frank Lucas, James Field, Louise Latham, Harry Bergman, Kathleen Phelan, Gilbert Milton, Edwin Whitner, Joe Walker, Michael Dolan, Dolores Walker, John Maddox, Sadie French, Sam Brunstein, Tommy Wright, Joe Parker, Joan Breymer, Harriet Slaughter, Eddie Gale, Morgan Wilson, Charlie West and Fred Hoskins. Margo Jones directed.

Time: Summer. Not too long ago.
Place: A small town.

Inherit the Wind is not history. The events which took place in Dayton, Tennessee, during the scorching July of 1925 are clearly the genesis of this play. It has, however, an exodus entirely its own.

Only a handful of phrases have been taken from the actual transcript of the famous Scopes Trial. Some of the characters of the play are related to the colorful figures in that battle of giants; but they have life and language of their own—and, therefore, names of their own.

The greatest reporters and historians of the century have written millions of words about the "Monkey Trial." We are indebted to them for their brilliant reportage. And we are grateful to the late Arthur Garfield Hays, who recounted to us much of the unwritten vividness of the Dayton adventure from his own memory and experience.

The collision of Bryan and Darrow at Dayton was dramatic, but it was not a drama. Moreover, the issues of their conflict have acquired new dimension and meaning in the thirty years since they clashed at the Rhea County Courthouse. So *Inherit the Wind* does not pretend to be journalism. It is theatre. It is not 1925. The stage directions set the time as "Not too long ago." It might have been yesterday. It could be tomorrow.

JEROME LAWRENCE
ROBERT E. LEE

ACT ONE

ACT ONE

SCENE I

In and around the Hillsboro Courthouse. The foreground is the actual courtroom, with jury box, judge's bench and a scattering of trial-scarred chairs and counsel tables. The back wall of the courtroom is non-existent. On a raked level above it is the courthouse square, the Main Street and the converging streets of the town. This is not so much a literal view of Hillsboro as it is an impression of a sleepy, obscure country town about to be vigorously awakened.

It is important to the concept of the play that the town is visible always, looming there, as much on trial as the individual defendant. The crowd is equally important throughout, so that the court becomes a cock-pit, an arena, with the active spectators on all sides of it.

It is an hour after dawn on a July day that promises to be a scorcher. HOWARD, a boy of thirteen, wanders onto the courthouse lawn. He is barefoot, wearing a pair of his pa's cut-down overalls. He carries an improvised fishing pole and a tin can. He studies the ground carefully, searching for something. A young girl's voice calls from off-stage.

MELINDA
(Calling sweetly)

How-ard! *(HOWARD, annoyed, turns and looks toward the voice. MELINDA, a healthy, pigtailed girl of twelve, skips on)* Hello, Howard.

(HOWARD is disinterested, continues to search the ground.)

HOWARD

'Lo, Lindy.

MELINDA
(Making conversation)

I think it's gonna be hotter'n yesterday. That rain last night didn't do much good.

HOWARD
(Professionally)

It brought up the worms. *(Suddenly he spots one in the lawn. Swiftly he grabs for it, and holds it up proudly)* Lookit this fat one!

MELINDA
(Shivering)

How can you touch 'em? It makes me all goose-bumpy!
(HOWARD dangles it in front of her face. She backs away, shuddering.)

HOWARD

What're yuh skeered of? *You* was a worm once!

MELINDA
(Shocked)

I wasn't neither!

HOWARD

You was so! When the whole world was covered with water, there was nuthin' but worms and blobs of jelly. And you and your whole family was worms!

MELINDA

We was not!.

HOWARD

Blobs of jelly, then.

MELINDA

Howard Blair, that's sinful talk! I'm gonna tell my pa and he'll make you wash your mouth out with soap!

HOWARD

Ahhh, your old man's a monkey! (MELINDA *gasps. She turns indignantly and runs off.* HOWARD *shrugs in the manner of a man-of-the-world*) 'Bye, Lindy. (*He deposits the worm in his tin can, and continues looking for more.* RACHEL *enters. She is twenty-two, pretty, but not beautiful. She wears a cotton summer dress. She carries a small composition-paper suitcase. There is a tense, distraught air about her. She may have been crying. She looks about nervously, as if she doesn't want to be seen. When she sees* HOWARD, *she hesitates; then she crosses quickly downstage into the courthouse area in the hope that the boy will not notice her. But he does see* RACHEL, *and watches her with puzzled curiosity. Then he spots another worm, tugs it out of the ground, and holds it up, wriggling.* HOWARD *addresses the worm*) What do you wanta be when you grow up?

(RACHEL *stands uncertainly in the courthouse area. This is strange ground to her. Unsure, she looks about.*)

RACHEL
(*Tentatively, calling*)

Mr. Meeker . . . ?

(*After a pause, a door at stage right opens.* MR. MEEKER, *the bailiff, enters. There is no collar on his shirt; his hair is tousled, and there is shaving soap on his face, which he is wiping off with a towel as he enters.*)

MEEKER
(*A little irritably*)

Who is it? (*Surprised*) Why, hello, Rachel. 'Scuse the way I look. (*He wipes the soap out of his ear. Then he notices her suitcase*) Not goin' away, are you? Excitement's just startin'.

RACHEL
(*Earnestly*)

Mr. Meeker, don't let my father know I came here.

MEEKER
(Shrugs)
The Reverend don't tell me his business. Don't know why
I should tell him mine.

RACHEL
I want to see Bert Cates. Is he all right?

MEEKER
Don't know why he shouldn't be. I always figured the
safest place in the world is a jail.

RACHEL
Can I go down and see him?

MEEKER
Ain't a very proper place for a minister's daughter.

RACHEL
I only want to see him for a minute.

MEEKER
Sit down, Rachel. I'll bring him up. You can talk to him
right here in the courtroom. (RACHEL *sits in one of the stiff
wooden chairs.* MEEKER *starts out, then pauses*) Long as I've
been bailiff here, we've never had nothin' but drunks, va-
grants, couple of chicken thieves. (*A little dreamily*) Our
best catch was that fella from Minnesota that chopped up
his wife; we had to extradite him. (*Shakes his head*) Seems
kinda queer havin' a schoolteacher in our jail. (*Shrugs*)
Might improve the writin' on the walls.
　(MEEKER *goes out. Nervously,* RACHEL *looks around at
the cold, official furnishings of the courtroom.* MEEKER *returns to the courtroom, followed by* BERT CATES. CATES
*is a pale, thin young man of twenty-four. He is quiet, shy,
well-mannered, not particularly good-looking.* RACHEL

and CATES *face each other expressionlessly, without speaking.* MEEKER *pauses in the doorway.*)

MEEKER

I'll leave you two alone to talk. Don't run off, Bert.
(MEEKER *goes out.* RACHEL *and* CATES *look at each other.*)

RACHEL

Hello, Bert.

CATES

Rache, I told you not to come here.

RACHEL

I couldn't help it. Nobody saw me. Mr. Meeker won't tell. (*Troubled*) I keep thinking of you, locked up here—

CATES
(*Trying to cheer her up*)

You know something funny? The food's better than the boarding house. And you'd better not tell anybody how cool it is down there, or we'll have a crime wave every summer.

RACHEL

I stopped by your place and picked up some of your things. A clean shirt, your best tie, some handkerchiefs.

CATES

Thanks.

RACHEL
(*Rushing to him*)

Bert, why don't you tell 'em it was all a joke? Tell 'em you didn't mean to break a law, and you won't do it again!

CATES

I suppose everybody's all steamed up about Brady coming.

RACHEL

He's coming in on a special train out of Chattanooga. Pa's going to the station to meet him. Everybody is!

CATES

Strike up the band.

RACHEL

Bert, it's still not too late. Why can't you admit you're wrong? If the biggest man in the country—next to the President, maybe—if Matthew Harrison Brady comes here to tell the whole world how wrong you are—

CATES

You still think I did wrong?

RACHEL

Why did you do it?

CATES

You know why I did it. I had the book in my hand, Hunter's *Civic Biology.* I opened it up, and read my sophomore science class Chapter 17, Darwin's *Origin of Species.* (RACHEL *starts to protest*) All it says is that man wasn't just stuck here like a geranium in a flower pot; that living comes from a *long* miracle, it didn't just happen in seven days.

RACHEL

There's a law against it.

CATES

I know that.

RACHEL

Everybody says what you did is bad.

CATES

It isn't as simple as that. Good or bad, black or white, night or day. Do you know, at the top of the world the twilight is six months long?

RACHEL

But we don't live at the top of the world. We live in Hillsboro, and when the sun goes down, it's dark. And why do you try to make it different? (RACHEL *gets the shirt, tie, and handkerchiefs from the suitcase*) Here.

CATES

Thanks, Rache.

RACHEL

Why can't you be on the right side of things?

CATES

Your father's side. (RACHEL *starts to leave.* CATES *runs after her*) Rache—love me!
　　(*They embrace.* MEEKER *enters with a long-handled broom.*)

MEEKER
(*Clears his throat*)

I gotta sweep.
　　(RACHEL *breaks away and hurries off.*)

CATES
(*Calling*)

Thanks for the shirt!
　　(MEEKER, *who has been sweeping impassively now stops and leans on the broom.*)

MEEKER

Imagine. Matthew Harrison Brady, comin' here. I voted for him for President. Twice. In nineteen hundred, and again in oh-eight. Wasn't old enough to vote for him the first time he ran. But my pa did. (*Turns proudly to* CATES) I *seen* him once. At a Chautauqua meeting in Chattanooga. (*Impressed, remembering*) The tent-poles shook! (CATES *moves nervously*) Who's gonna be your lawyer, son?

> CATES

I don't know yet. I wrote to that newspaper in Baltimore. They're sending somebody.

> MEEKER
> (*Resumes sweeping*)

He better be loud.

> CATES
> (*Picking up the shirt*)

You want me to go back down?

> MEEKER

No need. You can stay up here if you want.

> CATES
> (*Going toward the jail*)

I'm supposed to be in jail; I'd better be in jail!
(MEEKER *shrugs and follows* CATES *off. The lights fade in the courtroom area, and come up on the town: morning of a hot July day. The* STOREKEEPER *enters, unlocking his store.* MRS. KREBS *saunters across the square.*)

> STOREKEEPER

Warm enough for you, Mrs. Krebs?

> MRS. KREBS

The Good Lord guv us the heat, and the Good Lord guv us the glands to sweat with.

> STOREKEEPER

I bet the Devil ain't so obliging.

MRS. KREBS

Don't intend to find out.
(*The* REVEREND JEREMIAH BROWN, *a gaunt, thin-lipped man, strides on. He looks around, scowling.*)

STOREKEEPER

Good morning, Reverend.

BROWN

'Morning.

MRS. KREBS

'Morning, Reverend.

BROWN

Mrs. Krebs. (*Shouting off*) Where's the banner? Why haven't you raised the banner?

CORKIN

(*Entering, followed by another workman*)
Paint didn't dry 'til jist now.
(*They are carrying a rolled-up canvas banner.*)

BROWN

See that you have it up before Mr. Brady arrives.
(COOPER *enters, gestures "hello" to the others.*)

CORKIN

Fast as we can do it, Reverend.

BROWN

We must show him at once what kind of a community this is.

CORKIN

Yes, Reverend. Come on, Phil. Hep.
(*They rig the banner to halyards between the buildings.*)

MRS. KREBS

Big day, Reverend.

CORKIN

Indeed it is. Picnic lunch ready, Mrs. Krebs?

MRS. KREBS

Fitt'n fer a king.
(BANNISTER, PLATT *and other townspeople gather ex-citedly. They are colorful small-town citizens, but not cari-catured rubes.*)

BOLLINGER
(*Running on, carrying his cornet*)
Station master says old 94's on time out of Chattanooga.
And Brady's on board all right!

COOPER

The minute Brady gets here, people gonna pour in. Town's gonna fill up like a rain barrel in a flood.

STOREKEEPER

That means business!
(MELINDA *and her mother come on and set up a lemon-ade stand.*)

BANNISTER

Where they gonna stay? Where we gonna sleep all them people?

MRS. KREBS

They got money, we'll sleep 'em.

PLATT

Looks like the biggest day for this town since we put up Coxey's army!

HOWARD
(*Bolting on*)
Hey! Ted Finney's got out his big bass drum. And y'oughta

see what they done to the depot! Ribbons all over the rainspouts!

MELINDA
Lemonade! Lemonade!
(The workmen hoist the banner above the heads of the crowd, where it hangs for the remainder of the action. The banner blares: "READ YOUR BIBLE.")

CORKIN
It's all ready, Reverend.
(The townspeople applaud. BOLLINGER toots a ragged fanfare. A HAWKER in a white apron wheels on a hot-dog stand. The crowd mills about, in holiday spirit.)

HAWKER
Hot dogs! Get your red-hots! Hot dogs!
(MRS. MCCLAIN enters with a shopping bag full of frond fans.)

MRS. MCCLAIN
Get your fans. Compliments of Maley's Funeral Home. Thirty-five cents.
(The stage is now full of eager and expectant people. MRS. BLAIR shoves her way through the crowd, looking for her son.)

MRS. BLAIR
(Calling)
Howard. Howard!

HOWARD
(Racing to her)
Hey, Ma. This is just like the county fair.

MRS. BLAIR
Now you settle down and stop runnin' around and pay some attention when Mr. Brady gets here. Spit down

your hair. (HOWARD *spits in her hand, and she pastes down a cowlick*) Hold still!

(HOWARD *flashes off through the crowd.* ELIJAH, *a "holy man" from the hills, comes on with a wooden vegetable crate full of books. He is bearded, wild-haired, dressed in a tattered burlap smock. His feet are bare. He sets up shop between the hot dogs and the lemonade, with a placard reading:* "WHERE WILL YOU SPEND ETERNITY?")

ELIJAH
(*In a shrill, screeching voice*)
Buy a Bible! Your guidebook to eternal life!

(E. K. HORNBECK *wanders on, carrying a suitcase. He is a newspaperman in his middle thirties, who sneers politely at everything, including himself. His clothes—those of a sophisticated city-dweller—contrast sharply with the attire of the townspeople.* HORNBECK *looks around, with wonderful contempt.*)

MRS. MCCLAIN
(*To* HORNBECK)
Want a fan? Compliments of Maley's Funeral Home—thirty-five cents!

HORNBECK
I'd die first.

MRS. KREBS
(*Unctuously, to* HORNBECK)
You're a stranger, aren't you, mister? Want a nice clean place to stay?

HORNBECK
I had a nice clean place to stay, madame,
And I left it to come here.

MRS. KREBS
(*Undaunted*)
You're gonna need a room.

HORNBECK

I have a reservation at the Mansion House.

MRS. KREBS

Oh? (*She sniffs*) That's all right, I suppose, for them as *likes* havin' a privy practically in the bedroom!

HORNBECK

The unplumbed and plumbing-less depths!
Ahhhh, Hillsboro—Heavenly Hillsboro.
The buckle on the Bible Belt.
> (*The* HAWKER *and* ELIJAH *converge on* HORNBECK *from opposite sides.*)

HAWKER

Hot dog?

ELIJAH

Bible?
> (HORNBECK *up-ends his suitcase and sits on it.*)

HORNBECK

Now that poses a pretty problem!
Which is hungrier—my stomach or my soul?
> (HORNBECK *buys a hot dog.*)

ELIJAH
(*Miffed*)
Are you an Evolutionist? An infidel? A sinner?

HORNBECK
(*Munching the hog dog*)
The worst kind. I write for a newspaper.
> (HORNBECK *offers his hand*)
I'm E. K. Hornbeck, Baltimore *Herald.*
I don't believe I caught your name . . . ?

ELIJAH
(*Impressively*)
They call me . . . Elijah.

HORNBECK
(Pleased)

Elijah! Yes! Why, I had no idea you were still around.
I've read some of your stuff.

ELIJAH
(Haughtily)

I neither read nor write.

HORNBECK

Oh. Excuse me.
I must be thinking of another Elijah.
(An ORGAN-GRINDER *enters, with a live monkey on a
string.* HORNBECK *spies the monkey gleefully; he greets
the monk with arms outstretched)*

Grandpa!
*(Crosses to the monkey, bends down and shakes the mon-
key's hand)*

Welcome to Hillsboro, sir!
Have you come to testify for the defense
Or for the prosecution?
(The monkey, oddly enough, doesn't answer)
No comment?

That's fairly safe. But I warn you, sir,
You can't compete with all these monkeyshines.
(MELINDA hands the monkey a penny.)

MELINDA

Look. He took my penny.

HORNBECK

How could you ask for better proof than that?
There's the father of the human race!

TIMMY
(Running on, breathlessly)

Train's coming! I seen the smoke 'way up the track!
(The train whistle sounds, off.)

BROWN
(Taking command)

All the members of the Bible League, get ready! Let us show Mr. Brady the spirit in which we welcome him to Hillsboro.

(MRS. BLAIR blows her pitch pipe and the townspeople parade off singing "Marching to Zion." Even the ORGAN-GRINDER leaves his monkey tied to the hurdy-gurdy and joins the departing crowd. But HORNBECK stays behind.)

HORNBECK

Amen.
(To the monkey)

Shield your eyes, monk!
You're about to meet the mightiest of your descendents.
A man who wears a cathedral for a cloak,
A church spire for a hat,
Whose tread has the thunder of the legions of the Lion-
    Hearted!

(The STOREKEEPER emerges from his establishment and looks in his own store window. HORNBECK turns to him)

You're missing the show.

STOREKEEPER

Somebody's got to mind the store.

HORNBECK

May I ask your opinion, sir, on Evolution?

STOREKEEPER

Don't have any opinions. They're bad for business.
(Off-stage, a cheer. Then the thumping drum into "Gimme That Old-Time Religion" sung by the unseen townspeople.)

HORNBECK
(To the monkey)

Sound the trumpet, beat the drum.
Everybody's come to town

To see your competition, monk.
Alive and breathing in the county cooler:
A high-school teacher—wild, untamed!
> (*The crowd surges back, augmented, in a jubilant parade.
> Many are carrying banners, reading:*

ARE YOU A MAN OR A MONKEY?
AMEND THE CONSTITUTION — PROHIBIT DARWIN
SAVE OUR SCHOOLS FROM SIN
MY ANCESTORS AIN'T APES!
WELCOME MATTHEW HARRISON BRADY
DOWN WITH DARWIN
BE A SWEET ANGEL
DON'T MONKEY WITH OUR SCHOOLS!
DARWIN IS WRONG!
DOWN WITH EVOLUTION
SWEETHEART, COME UNTO THE LORD

> HORNBECK *goes to the background to watch the show.*
> MATTHEW HARRISON BRADY *comes on, a benign gi-
> ant of a man, wearing a pith helmet. He basks in the
> cheers and the excitement, like a patriarch surrounded by
> his children. He is gray, balding, paunchy, an indetermi-
> nate sixty-five. He is followed by* MRS. BRADY; *the*
> MAYOR; REVEREND BROWN; TOM DAVENPORT, *the
> circuit district attorney; some newspapermen, and an army
> of the curious.*)

ALL
(*Singing*)

Gimme that old-time religion,
Gimme that old-time religion,
Gimme that old-time religion,
It's good enough for me!

It was good enough for father,
It was good enough for father,
It was good enough for father,
And it's good enough for me!

* * *

It was good for the Hebrew children,
It was good for the Hebrew children,
It was good for the Hebrew children,
And it's good enough for me!

Gimme that old-time religion,
Gimme that old-time religion,
Gimme that old-time religion,
It's good enough for me!

MAYOR
(*Speaks*)

Mr. Brady, if you please.

REVEREND
(*Singing*)

It is good enough for Brady.

CROWD

It is good enough for Brady,
It is good enough for Brady,
And it's good enough for me!
(*Cheers and applause.* BRADY *seems to carry with him a built-in spotlight. So* MRS. BRADY—*pretty, fashionably dressed, a proper "Second Lady" to the nation's "Second Man"—seems always to be in his shadow. This does not annoy her.* SARAH BRADY *is content that all her thoughts and emotions should gain the name of action through her husband.* BRADY *removes his hat and raises his hand. Obediently, the crowd falls to a hushed anticipatory silence.*)

BRADY

Friends—and I can see most of you are my friends, from the way you have decked out your beautiful city of Hillsboro—(*There is a pleased reaction, and a spattering of applause. When* BRADY *speaks, there can be no doubt of his personal magnetism. Even* HORNBECK, *who slouches contemptuously at far left, is impressed with the speaker's power;*

for here is a man to be reckoned with) Mrs. Brady and I are delighted to be among you! (BRADY *takes his wife's hand and draws her to his side)* I could only wish one thing: that you had not given us quite so warm a welcome! (BRADY *removes his alpaca coat. The crowd laughs.* BRADY *beams.* MRS. MCCLAIN *hands him a frond fan.* BRADY *takes it)* Bless you. (*He fans himself vigorously)* My friends of Hillsboro, you know why I have come here. I have not come merely to prosecute a lawbreaker, an arrogant youth who has spoken out against the Revealed Word. I have come because what has happened in a schoolroom of your town has unloosed a wicked attack from the big cities of the North!—an attack upon the law which you have so wisely placed among the statutes of this state. I am here to defend that which is most precious in the hearts of all of us: the Living Truth of the Scriptures!

(*Applause and emotional cheering.*)

PHOTOGRAPHER
Mr. Brady. Mr. Brady, a picture?

BRADY
I shall be happy to oblige! (*The townspeople, chanting "Go Tell It on the Mountain," move upstage.* BRADY *begins to organize a group photograph. To his wife)* Sarah . . .

MRS. BRADY
(*Moving out of the camera range)*
No, Matt. Just you and the dignitaries.

BRADY
You are the Mayor, are you not?

MAYOR
(*Stepping forward, awkwardly)*
I am, sir.

BRADY
(Extending his hand)
My name is Matthew Harrison Brady.

MAYOR
Oh, I know. Everybody knows that. I had a speech of welcome ready, but somehow it didn't seem necessary.

BRADY
I shall be honored to hear your greeting, sir.
(The MAYOR clears his throat and takes some notes from his pocket.)

MAYOR
(Sincerely)
Mr. Matthew Harrison Brady, this municipality is proud to have within its city limits the warrior who has always fought for us ordinary people. The lady folks of this town wouldn't have the vote if it wasn't for you, fightin' to give 'em all that suffrage. Mr. President Wilson wouldn't never have got to the White House and won the war if it wasn't for you supportin' him. And, in conclusion, the Governor of our state . . .

PHOTOGRAPHER
Hold it! *(The camera clicks)* Thank you.
(MRS. BRADY is disturbed by the informality of the pose.)

MRS. BRADY
Matt—you didn't have your coat on.

BRADY
(To the PHOTOGRAPHER)
Perhaps we should have a more formal pose. *(As MRS. BRADY helps him on with his coat)* Who is the spiritual leader of the community?

MAYOR

That would be the Reverend Jeremiah Brown.
(REVEREND BROWN *steps forward.*)

BROWN

Your servant, and the Lord's.
(BRADY *and* BROWN *shake hands.*)

BRADY

The Reverend at my left, the Mayor at my right. (*Stiffly, they face the camera*) We must look grave, gentlemen, but not too serious. Hopeful, I think is the word. We must look hopeful.
(BRADY *assumes the familiar oratorical pose. The camera clicks. Unnoticed, the barefoot* HOWARD *has stuck his head, mouth agape, into the picture. The* MAYOR *refers to the last page of his undelivered speech.*)

MAYOR

In conclusion, the Governor of our state has vested in me the authority to confer upon you a commission as Honorary Colonel in the State Militia.
(*Applause.*)

BRADY
(*Savoring it*)
"Colonel Brady." I like the sound of that!

BROWN

We thought you might be hungry, Colonel Brady, after your train ride.

MAYOR

So the members of our Ladies' Aid have prepared a buffet lunch.

BRADY

Splendid, splendid—I could do with a little snack.

(Some of the townspeople, at BROWN'S *direction, carry on a long picnic table, loaded with foodstuffs, potato salad, fried turkey, pickled fruits, cold meats and all the picnic paraphernalia.* RACHEL *comes on following the table, carrying a pitcher of lemonade which she places on the table.)*

BANNISTER
(An eager beaver)

You know, Mr. Brady—Colonel Brady—all of us here voted for you three times.

BRADY

I trust it was in three separate elections!
(There is laughter. TOM DAVENPORT, *a crisp, business-like young man, offers his hand to* BRADY.)

DAVENPORT

Sir, I'm Tom Davenport.

BRADY
(Beaming)

Of course. Circuit district attorney. *(Putting his arm around* DAVENPORT'S *shoulder)* We'll be a team, won't we, young man! Quite a team! *(The picnic table is in place. The sight of the food being uncovered is a magnetic attraction to Brady. He beams, and moistens his lips)* Ahhhh, what a handsome repast! *(Some of the women grin sheepishly at the flattery.* BRADY *is a great eater, and he piles mountains of food on his plate)* What a challenge it is, to fit on the old armor again! To test the steel of our Truth against the blasphemies of Science! To stand—

MRS. BRADY

Matthew, it's a warm day. Remember, the doctor told you not to overeat.

BRADY

Don't worry, Mother. Just a bite or two. *(He hoists a huge*

drumstick on his plate, then assails a mountain of potato salad)
Who among you knows the defendant?—Cates, is that
his name?

DAVENPORT
Well, we *all* know him, sir.

MAYOR
Just about everybody in Hillsboro knows everybody else.

BRADY
Can someone tell me—is this fellow Cates a criminal by
nature?

RACHEL
(Almost involuntarily)
Bert isn't a criminal. He's good, really. He's just—
*(RACHEL seems to shrink from the attention that centers
on her. She takes an empty bowl and starts off with it.)*

BRADY
Wait, my child. Is Mr. Cates your friend?

RACHEL
(Looking down, trying to get away)
I can't tell you anything about him—

BROWN
(Fiercely)
Rachel! *(To BRADY)* My daughter will be pleased to an-
swer any questions about Bertram Cates.

BRADY
Your daughter, Reverend? You must be proud, indeed.
*(BROWN nods. BRADY takes a mouthful of potato salad,
turns to RACHEL)* Now. How did you come to be ac-
quainted with Mr. Cates?

RACHEL
(*Suffering*)
At school. I'm a schoolteacher, too.

BRADY
I'm sure you teach according to the precepts of the Lord.

RACHEL
I try. My pupils are only second-graders.

BRADY
Has Mr. Cates ever tried to pollute your mind with his heathen dogma?

RACHEL
Bert isn't a heathen!

BRADY
(*Sympathetically*)
I understand your loyalty, my child. This man, the man in your jailhouse, is a fellow schoolteacher. Likable, no doubt. And you are loath to speak out against him before all these people. (BRADY *takes her arm, still carrying his plate. He moves her easily away from the others. As they move*) Think of me as a friend, Rachel. And tell me what troubles you.
　　(BRADY *moves her upstage and their conversation continues, inaudible to us.* BRADY *continues to eat,* RACHEL *speaks to him earnestly. The townspeople stand around the picnic table, munching the buffet lunch.*)

BANNISTER
Who's gonna be the defense attorney?

DAVENPORT
We don't know yet. It hasn't been announced.

MAYOR
(He hands a modest picnic plate to MRS. BRADY)
Whoever it is, he won't have much of a chance against your husband, will he, Mrs. Brady?
(There are chortles of self-confident amusement. But HORNBECK saunters toward the picnic table.)

HORNBECK
I disagree.

MAYOR
Who are you?

HORNBECK
Hornbeck. E. K. Hornbeck, of the Baltimore *Herald*.

BROWN
(Can't quite place the name, but it has unpleasant connotations)
Hornbeck . . . Hornbeck . . .

HORNBECK
I am a newspaperman, bearing news.
When this sovereign state determined to indict
The sovereign mind of a less-than-sovereign schoolteacher,
My editors decided there was more than a headline here.
The Baltimore *Herald*, therefore, is happy to announce
That it is sending two representatives to "Heavenly Hillsboro":
The most brilliant reporter in America today,
Myself.
And.
And the most agile legal mind of the Twentieth Century,
Henry Drummond.
(This name is like a whip-crack.)

MRS. BRADY
(Stunned)
Drummond!

BROWN

Henry Drummond, the agnostic?

BANNISTER

I heard about him. He got those two Chicago child murderers off just the other day.

BROWN

A vicious, godless man!
(Blithely, HORNBECK reaches across the picnic table and chooses a drumstick. He waves it jauntily toward the astonished party.)

HORNBECK

A Merry Christmas and a Jolly Fourth of July!
(Munching the drumstick, HORNBECK goes off. Unnoticed, BRADY and RACHEL have left the scene, missing this significant disclosure. There is a stunned pause.)

DAVENPORT
(Genuinely impressed)
Henry Drummond for the defense. Well!

BROWN

Henry Drummond is an agent of darkness. *(With resolution)* We won't let him in the town!

DAVENPORT

I don't know by what law you could keep him out.

MAYOR
(Rubbing his chin)
I'll look it up in the town ordinances.

BROWN

I saw Drummond once. In a courtroom in Ohio. A man was on trial for a most brutal crime. Although he knew—and admitted—the man was guilty, Drummond was perverting the evidence to cast the guilt away from the accused and onto you and me and all of society.

MRS. BRADY

Henry Drummond. Oh, dear me.

BROWN

I can still see him. A slouching hulk of a man, whose head juts out like an animal's. (*He imitates* DRUMMOND'S *slouch.* MELINDA *watches, frightened*) You look into his face, and you wonder why God made such a man. And then you know that God didn't make him, that he is a creature of the Devil, perhaps even the Devil himself!

(*Little* MELINDA *utters a frightened cry, and buries her head in the folds of her mother's skirt.* BRADY *re-enters with* RACHEL, *who has a confused and guilty look.* BRADY'S *plate has been scraped clean; only the fossil of the turkey leg remains. He looks at the ring of faces, which have been disturbed by* BROWN'S *description of the heretic* DRUMMOND. MRS. BRADY *comes toward him.*)

MRS. BRADY

Matt—they're bringing Henry Drummond for the defense.

BRADY
(*Pale*)

Drummond? (*The townspeople are impressed by the impact of this name on* BRADY) Henry Drummond!

BROWN

We won't allow him in the town!

MAYOR
(*Lamely*)

I think—maybe the Board of Health—
(*He trails off.*)

BRADY
(*Crossing thoughtfully*)

No. (*He turns*) I believe we should *welcome* Henry Drummond.

MAYOR
(Astonished)

Welcome him!

BRADY

If the enemy sends its Goliath into battle, it magnifies our cause. Henry Drummond has stalked the courtrooms of this land for forty years. When he fights, headlines follow. *(With growing fervor)* The whole world will be watching our victory over Drummond. *(Dramatically)* If St. George had slain a dragonfly, who would remember him.

    (Cheers and pleased reactions from the crowd.)

MRS. BLAIR

Would you care to finish off the pickled apricots, Mr. Brady?

    (BRADY takes them.)

BRADY

It would be a pity to see them go to waste.

MRS. BRADY

Matt, do you think—

BRADY

Have to build up my strength, Mother, for the battle ahead. *(Munching thoughtfully)* Now what will Drummond do? He'll try to make us forget the lawbreaker and put the law on trial. *(He turns to RACHEL)* But we'll have the *answer* for Mr. Drummond. Right here, in some of the things this sweet young lady has told me.

RACHEL

But Mr. Brady—

    (BRADY turns to BROWN.)

BRADY

A fine girl, Reverend. Fine girl!

    (RACHEL seems tormented, but helpless.)

BROWN

Rachel has always been taught to do the righteous thing.
(RACHEL *moves off.*)

BRADY

I'm sure she has.
(MELINDA *hands him a glass of lemonade.*)

BRADY

Thank you. A toast, then! A toast to tomorrow! To the beginning of the trial and the success of our cause. A toast, in good American lemonade!
(*He stands lifting his glass. Others rise and join the toast.* BRADY *downs his drink.*)

MRS. BRADY

Mr. Mayor, it's time now for Mr. Brady's nap. He always likes to nap after a meal.

MAYOR

We have a suite ready for you at the Mansion House. I think you'll find your bags already there.

BRADY

Very thoughtful, considerate of you.

MAYOR

If you'll come with me—it's only across the square.

BRADY

I want to thank all the members of the Ladies' Aid for preparing this nice little picnic repast.

MRS. KREBS
(*Beaming*)

Our pleasure, sir.

BRADY

And if I seemed to pick at my food, I don't want you to

think I didn't enjoy it. (*Apologetically*) But you see, we had a box lunch on the train.

> (*There is a good-humored reaction to this, and the* BRADYS *move off accompanied by the throng of admirers, singing "It is good enough for Brady." Simultaneously the lights fade down on the courthouse lawn and fade up on the courtroom area.* HORNBECK *saunters on, chewing at an apple. He glances about the courtroom as if he were searching for something. When* RACHEL *hurries on,* HORNBECK *drops back into a shadow and she does not see him.*)

RACHEL
(*Distressed*)

Mr. Meeker. Mr. Meeker? (*She calls down toward the jail*) Bert, can you hear me? Bert, you've got to tell me what to do. I don't know what to do—

> (HORNBECK *takes a bite out of his apple.* RACHEL *turns sharply at the sound, surprised to find someone else in the courtroom.*)

HORNBECK
(*Quietly*)

I give advice, at remarkably low hourly rates.
Ten percent off to unmarried young ladies,
And special discounts to the clergy and their daughters.

RACHEL

What are you doing here?

HORNBECK

I'm inspecting the battlefield
The night before the battle. Before it's cluttered
With the debris of journalistic camp-followers.
> (*Hiking himself up on a window ledge*)
I'm scouting myself an observation post
To watch the fray.
> (RACHEL *starts to go off*)
Wait. Why do you want to see Bert Cates?

What's he to you, or you to him?
Can it be that both beauty and biology
Are on our side?

> *(Again she starts to leave. But* HORNBECK *jumps down from his ledge and crosses toward her)*

There's a newspaper here I'd like to have you see.
It just arrived
From that wicked modern Sodom and Gomorrah,
Baltimore!

> *(*RACHEL *looks at him quizzically as he fishes a tear sheet out of his pocket)*

Not the entire edition, of course.
No Happy Hooligan, Barney Google, Abe Kabibble.
Merely the part worth reading: E. K. Hornbeck's
Brilliant little symphony of words.

> *(He offers her the sheet, but she doesn't take it)*

You should read it.

> *(Almost reluctantly, she starts to read)*

                                        My typewriter's been singing
A sweet, sad song about the Hillsboro heretic,
B. Cates: boy-Socrates, latter-day Dreyfus,
Romeo with a biology book.

> *(He looks over her shoulder, admiring his own writing. He takes another bite out of the apple)*

I may be rancid butter,
But I'm on your side of the bread.

RACHEL
> *(Looking up, surprised)*

This sounds as if you're a friend of Bert's.

HORNBECK
As much as a critic can be a friend to anyone.

> *(He sits backward on a chair, watching her head. He takes another bite out of his apple, then offers it to her)*

Have a bite?

> *(*RACHEL, *busily reading, shakes her head)*

Don't worry. I'm not the serpent, Little Eva.
This isn't from the Tree of Knowledge.

You won't find one in the orchards of Heavenly Hillsboro.
Birches, beeches, butternuts. A few ignorance bushes.
No Tree of Knowledge.

*(RACHEL has finished reading the copy; and she looks up
at HORNBECK with a new respect.)*

RACHEL

Will this be published here, in the local paper?

HORNBECK

In the "Weekly Bugle"? Or whatever it is they call
The leaden stuff they blow through the local linotypes?
I doubt it.

RACHEL

It would help Bert if the people here could read this. It
would help them understand . . . ! *(She appraises HORN-
BECK, puzzled)* I never would have expected you to write
an article like this. You seem so—

HORNBECK

Cynical? That's my fascination.
I do hateful things, for which people love me,
And lovable things for which they hate me.
I am a friend of enemies, the enemy of friends;
I am admired for my detestability.
I am both Poles and the Equator,
With no Temperate Zones between.

RACHEL

You make it sound as if Bert is a hero. I'd like to think
that, but I can't. A schoolteacher is a public servant: I
think he should do what the law and the school-board
want him to. If the superintendent says, "Miss Brown,
you're to teach from Whitley's *Second Reader,*" I don't feel
I have to give him an argument.

HORNBECK

Ever give your pupils a snap-quiz on existence?

RACHEL

What?

HORNBECK

Where we came from, where we are, where we're going?

RACHEL

All the answers to those questions are in the Bible.

HORNBECK
(With a genuine incredulity)

All?! You feed the youth of Hillsboro
From the little truck-garden of your mind?

RACHEL
(Offended, angry)

I think there must be something wrong in what Bert believes, if a great man like Mr. Brady comes here to speak out against him.

HORNBECK

Matthew Harrison Brady came here
To find himself a stump to shout from.
That's all.

RACHEL

You couldn't understand. Mr. Brady is the champion of ordinary people, like us.

HORNBECK

Wake up, Sleeping Beauty. The ordinary people
Played a dirty trick on Colonel Brady.
They ceased to exist.
    (RACHEL looks puzzled)
                    Time was
When Brady was the hero of the hinterland,
Water-boy for the great unwashed.
But they've got inside plumbing in their heads these days!
There's a highway through the backwoods now,

And the trees of the forest have reluctantly made room
For their leafless cousins, the telephone poles.
Henry's Lizzie rattles into town
And leaves behind
The Yesterday-Messiah,
Standing in the road alone
In a cloud of flivver dust.
   (*Emphatically, he brandishes the apple*)
The boob has been de-boobed.
Colonel Brady's virginal small-towner
Has been *had*—
By Marconi and Montgomery Ward.
   (HORNBECK *strolls out of the courtroom and onto the
   town square; the lights dissolve as before from one area to
   the other.* RACHEL *goes off in the darkness. The store
   fronts glow with sunset light. The* SHOPKEEPER *pulls the
   shade in his store window and locks the door.* MRS. MC-
   CLAIN *crosses, fanning herself wearily.*)

STOREKEEPER
Gonna be a hot night, Mrs. McClain.

MRS. MCCLAIN
I thought we'd get some relief when the sun went down.
   (HORNBECK *tosses away his apple core, then leans back
   and watches as the* SHOPKEEPER *and* MRS. MCCLAIN
   go off. The ORGAN-GRINDER *comes on, idly with his
   monkey.* MELINDA *enters attracted by the melody which
   tinkles in the twilight. She gives the monkey a penny. The*
   ORGAN-GRINDER *thanks her, and moves off.* MELINDA
   is alone, back to the audience, in center stage. HORN-
   BECK, *silent and motionless, watches from the side. The
   faces of the buildings are now red with the dying moment of
   sunset.*
   A long, ominous shadow appears across the buildings, cast from a figure approaching off stage.* MELINDA,
   awed, watches the shadow grow. HENRY DRUMMOND
   enters, carrying a valise. He is hunched over, head jutting

forward, exactly as BROWN *described him. The red of the sun behind him hits his slouching back, and his face is in shadow.* MELINDA *turns and looks at* DRUMMOND, *full in the face.)*

MELINDA
(Terrified)

It's the Devil!
(Screaming with fear MELINDA *runs off.* HORNBECK *crosses slowly toward* DRUMMOND, *and offers his hand.)*

HORNBECK

Hello, Devil. Welcome to Hell.

The lights fade

SCENE II

The courtroom. A few days later.

The townspeople are packed into the sweltering courtroom. The shapes of the buildings are dimly visible in the background, as if Hillsboro itself were on trial. Court is in session, fans are pumping. The humorless JUDGE sits at his bench; he has a nervous habit of flashing an automatic smile after every ruling. CATES sits beside DRUMMOND at a counsel table. BRADY sits grandly at another table, fanning himself with benign self-assurance. HORNBECK is seated on his window ledge. RA-CHEL, tense, is among the spectators. In the jury box, ten of the twelve jurors are already seated. BANNISTER is on the witness stand. DAVENPORT is examining him.

DAVENPORT
Do you attend church regularly, Mr. Bannister?

BANNISTER
Only on Sundays.

DAVENPORT
That's good enough for the prosecution. Your Honor, we will accept this man as a member of the jury.
    (BANNISTER *starts toward the jury box.*)

JUDGE
One moment, Mr. Bannister. You're not excused.

BANNISTER
(A little petulant)
I wanted that there front seat in the jury box.

DRUMMOND
(Rising)
Well, hold your horses, Bannister. You may get it yet!
(BANNISTER *returns to the witness chair.*)

JUDGE
Mr. Drummond, you may examine the venireman.

DRUMMOND
Thank you, Your Honor. Mr. Bannister, how come you're
so anxious to get that front seat over there?

BANNISTER
Everybody says this is going to be quite a show.

DRUMMOND
I hear the same thing. Ever read anything in a book about
Evolution?

BANNISTER
Nope.

DRUMMOND
Or about a fella named Darwin?

BANNISTER
Can't say I have.

DRUMMOND
I'll bet you read your Bible.

BANNISTER
Nope.

DRUMMOND
How come?

BANNISTER

Can't read.

DRUMMOND

Well, you are fortunate. (*There are a few titters through the courtroom*) He'll do.

(BANNISTER *turns toward the* JUDGE, *poised.*)

JUDGE

Take your seat, Mr. Bannister. (BANNISTER *races to the jury box as if shot from a gun, and sits in the remaining front seat, beaming*) Mr. Meeker, will you call a venireman to fill the twelfth and last seat on the jury?

BRADY
(*Rising*)

Your Honor, before we continue, will the court entertain a motion on a matter of procedure?

MEEKER
(*Calling toward the spectators*)

Jesse H. Dunlap. You're next, Jesse.

JUDGE

Will the learned prosecutor state the motion?

BRADY

It has been called to my attention that the temperature in this courtroom is now 97 degrees Fahrenheit. (*He mops his forehead with a large handkerchief*) And it may get hotter! (*There is laughter.* BRADY *basks in the warmth of his popularity*) I do not feel that the dignity of the court will suffer if we remove a few superfluous outer garments.

(BRADY *indicates his alpaca coat.*)

JUDGE

Does the defense have any objection to Colonel Brady's motion?

DRUMMOND
(*Askance*)

I don't know if the dignity of the court can be upheld with these galluses I've got on.

JUDGE

We'll take that chance, Mr. Drummond. Those who wish to remove their coats may do so.

(*With relief, many of the spectators take off their coats and loosen their collar buttons.* DRUMMOND *wears wide, bright purple suspenders. The spectators react.*)

BRADY
(*With affable sarcasm*)

Is the counsel for the defense showing us the latest fashion in the great metropolitan city of Chicago?

DRUMMOND
(*Pleased*)

Glad you asked me that. I brought these along special. (*He cocks his thumbs in the suspenders*) Just so happens I bought these galluses at Peabody's General Store in *your* home town, Mr. Brady. Weeping Water, Nebraska.

(DRUMMOND *snaps the suspenders jauntily. There is amused reaction at this.* BRADY *is nettled: this is his show, and he wants all the laughs. The* JUDGE *pounds for order.*)

JUDGE

Let us proceed with the selection of the final juror.

(MEEKER *brings* JESSE DUNLAP *to the stand. He is a rugged, righteous-looking man.*)

MEEKER

State your name and occupation.

DUNLAP

Jesse H. Dunlap. Farmer and cabinetmaker.

DAVENPORT

Do you believe in the Bible, Mr. Dunlap?

DUNLAP
(Vigorously)

I believe in the Holy Word of God. And I believe in
Matthew Harrison Brady!
(There is some applause, and a few scattered "Amens."
BRADY *waves acceptance.)*

DAVENPORT

This man is acceptable to the prosecution.

JUDGE

Very well, Mr. Drummond?

DRUMMOND
(Quietly, without rising)

No questions. Not acceptable.

BRADY
(Annoyed)

Does Mr. Drummond refuse this man a place on the jury
simply because he believes in the Bible?

DRUMMOND

If you find an Evolutionist in this town, you can refuse him.

BRADY
(Angrily)

I object to the defense attorney rejecting a worthy citizen
without so much as asking him a question!

DRUMMOND
(Agreeably)

All right. I'll ask him a question. *(Saunters over to* DUN-
LAP*)* How are you?

DUNLAP
(A little surprised)

Kinda hot.

DRUMMOND

So am I. Excused.
(DUNLAP *looks at the* JUDGE, *confused.*)

JUDGE

You are excused from jury duty, Mr. Dunlap. You may step down.
(DUNLAP *goes back and joins the spectators, a little miffed.*)

BRADY
(Piously)

I object to the note of levity which the counsel for the defense is introducing into these proceedings.

JUDGE

The bench agrees with you in spirit, Colonel Brady.

DRUMMOND
(Rising angrily)

And *I* object to all this damned "Colonel" talk. I am not familiar with Mr. Brady's military record.

JUDGE

Well—he was made an Honorary Colonel in our State Militia. The day he arrived in Hillsboro.

DRUMMOND

The use of this title prejudices the case of my client: it calls up a picture of the prosecution, astride a white horse, ablaze in the uniform of a militia colonel, with all the forces of right and righteousness marshaled behind him.

JUDGE

What can we do?

DRUMMOND

Break him. Make him a private. I have no serious objection to the honorary title of "Private Brady."
(There is a buzz of reaction. The JUDGE *gestures for the* MAYOR *to come over for a hurried, whispered conference.)*

MAYOR
(After some whispering)

Well, we can't take it back—! *(There is another whispered exchange. Then the* MAYOR *steps gingerly toward* DRUMMOND*)* By—by authority of—well, I'm sure the Governor won't have any objection—I hereby appoint you, Mr. Drummond, a temporary Honorary Colonel in the State Militia.

DRUMMOND
(Shaking his head, amused)

Gentlemen, what can I say? It is not often in a man's life that he attains the exalted rank of "temporary Honorary Colonel."

MAYOR

It will be made permanent, of course, pending the arrival of the proper papers over the Governor's signature.

DRUMMOND
(Looking at the floor)

I thank you.

JUDGE

Colonel Brady. Colonel Drummond. You will examine the next venireman.
*(*MEEKER *brings* GEORGE SILLERS *to the stand.)*

MEEKER

State your name and occupation.

SILLERS

George Sillers. I work at the feed store.

DAVENPORT

Tell me, sir. Would you call yourself a religious man?

SILLERS

I guess I'm as religious as the next man.
(BRADY *rises.* DAVENPORT *immediately steps back, deferring to his superior.*)

BRADY

In Hillsboro, sir, that means a great deal. Do you have any children, Mr. Sillers?

SILLERS

Not as I know of.

BRADY

If you had a son, Mr. Sillers, or a daughter, what would you think if that sweet child came home from school and told you that a Godless teacher—

DRUMMOND

Objection! We're supposed to be choosing jury members! The prosecution's denouncing the defendant before the trial has even begun!

JUDGE

Objection sustained.
(The JUDGE *and* BRADY *exchange meaningless smiles.*)

BRADY

Mr. Sillers. Do you have any personal opinions with regard to the defendant that might prejudice you on his behalf?

SILLERS

Cates? I don't hardly know him. He bought some peat moss from me once, and paid his bill.

BRADY

Mr. Sillers impresses me as an honest, God-fearing man. I accept him.

JUDGE

Thank you, Colonel Brady. *Colonel* Drummond?

DRUMMOND
(Strolling toward the witness chair)
Mr. Sillers, you just said you were a religious man. Tell me something. Do you work at it very hard?

SILLERS

Well, I'm pretty busy down at the feed store. My wife tends to the religion for both of us.

DRUMMOND

In other words, you take care of this life, and your wife takes care of the next one?

DAVENPORT

Objection.

JUDGE

Objection sustained.

DRUMMOND

While your wife was tending to the religion, Mr. Sillers, did you ever happen to bump into a fella named Charles Darwin?

SILLERS

Not till recent.

DRUMMOND

From what you've heard about this Darwin, do you think your wife would want to have him over for Sunday dinner?
(BRADY *rises magnificently.*)

BRADY

Your Honor, my worthy opponent from Chicago is cluttering the issue with hypothetical questions—

DRUMMOND
(*Wheeling*)

I'm doing *your* job, Colonel.

DAVENPORT
(*Leaping up*)

The prosecution is perfectly able to handle its own arguments.

DRUMMOND

Look, I've established that Mr. Sillers isn't working very hard at religion. Now, for your sake, I want to make sure he isn't working at Evolution.

SILLERS
(*Simply*)

I'm just working at the feed store.

DRUMMOND
(*To the* JUDGE)

This man's all right. (*Turning*) Take a box seat, Mr. Sillers.

BRADY

I am not altogether satisfied that Mr. Sillers will render impartial—

DRUMMOND

Out of order. The prosecution has already accepted this man.
(*The following becomes a simultaneous wrangle among the attorneys.*)

BRADY

I want a fair trial.

DRUMMOND

So do I!

BRADY

Unless the state of mind of the members of the jury conforms to the laws and patterns of society—

DRUMMOND

Conform! Conform! What do you want to do—run the jury through a meat-grinder, so they all come out the same?

DAVENPORT

Your Honor!

BRADY

I've seen what you can do to a jury. Twist and tangle them. Nobody's forgotten the Endicott Publishing case—where you made the jury believe the obscenity was in their own minds, not on the printed page. It was immoral what you did to that jury. Tricking them. Judgment by confusion. Think you can get away with it here?

DRUMMOND

All I want is to prevent the clock-stoppers from dumping a load of medieval nonsense into the United States Constitution.

JUDGE

This is not a Federal court.

DRUMMOND
(*Slapping his hand on the table*)
Well, dammit, you've got to stop 'em somewhere.
(*The* JUDGE *beats with his gavel.*)

JUDGE

Gentlemen, you are *both* out of order. The bench holds that the jury has been selected. (BRADY *lets his arms fall, with a gesture of sweet charity*) Because of the lateness of the hour and the unusual heat, the court is recessed until ten o'clock tomorrow morning. (JUDGE *raps the gavel, and the court begins to break up. Then the* JUDGE *notices a slip of paper, and raps for order again*) Oh. The Reverend Brown has asked me to make this announcement. There will be a prayer meeting tonight on the courthouse lawn, to pray for justice and guidance. All are invited.

DRUMMOND

Your Honor. I object to this commercial announcement.

JUDGE

Commercial announcement?

DRUMMOND

For Reverend Brown's product. Why don't you announce that there will be an Evolutionist meeting?

JUDGE

I have no knowledge of such a meeting.

DRUMMOND

That's understandable. It's bad enough that everybody coming into this courtroom has to walk underneath a banner that says: "Read Your Bible!" Your Honor, I want that sign taken down! Or else I want another one put up—just as big, just as big letters—saying "Read Your Darwin!"

JUDGE

That's preposterous!

DRUMMOND

It certainly is!

JUDGE

You are out of order, Colonel Drummond. The court stands recessed.

(As the formality of the courtroom is relaxed, there is a general feeling of relief. Spectators and jury members adjust their sticky clothes, and start moving off. Many of the townspeople gather around BRADY, *to shake his hand, get his autograph, and to stand for a moment in the great man's presence. They cluster about him, and follow* BRADY *as he goes off, the shepherd leading his flock. In marked contrast,* DRUMMOND *packs away his brief in a tattered leather case; but no one comes near him.* RACHEL *moves toward* BERT. *They stand face-to-face, wordlessly. Both seem to wish the whole painful turmoil were over. Suddenly,* RACHEL *darts to* DRUMMOND'S *side.* CATES *opens his mouth to stop her, but she speaks rapidly, with pent-up tension.)*

RACHEL

Mr. Drummond. You've got to call the whole thing off. It's not too late. Bert knows he did wrong. He didn't mean to. And he's sorry. Now why can't he just stand up and say to everybody: "I did wrong. I broke a law. I admit it. I won't do it again." Then they'd stop all this fuss, and—everything would be like it was.

*(*DRUMMOND *looks at* RACHEL, *not unkindly.)*

DRUMMOND

Who are you?

RACHEL

I'm—a friend of Bert's.
*(*DRUMMOND *turns to* CATES.*)*

DRUMMOND

How about it, boy? Getting cold feet?

CATES

I never thought it would be like this. Like Barnum and Bailey coming to town.

DRUMMOND
(Easily)
We can call it off. You want to quit?

RACHEL
(Coming to BERT'S *side)*
Yes!

CATES
People look at me as if I was a murderer. Worse than a
murderer! That fella from Minnesota who killed his
wife—remember, Rachel—half the town turned out to see
'em put him on the train. They just looked at him as if he
was a curiosity—not like they *hated* him! Not like he'd
done anything really wrong! Just different!

DRUMMOND
(Laughs a little to himself)
There's nothing very original about murdering your wife.

CATES
People I thought were my friends look at me now as if I
had horns growing out of my head.

DRUMMOND
You murder a wife, it isn't nearly as bad as murdering
an old wives' tale. Kill one of their fairy-tale notions,
and they call down the wrath of God, Brady, and the state
legislature.

RACHEL
You make a joke out of everything. You seem to think it's
so funny!

DRUMMOND
Lady, when you lose your power to laugh, you lose your
power to think straight.

CATES

Mr. Drummond, I can't laugh. I'm scared.

DRUMMOND

Good. You'd be a damned fool if you weren't.

RACHEL
(Bitterly)

You're supposed to help Bert; but every time you swear you make it worse for him.

DRUMMOND
(Honestly)

I'm sorry if I offend you. (He smiles) But I don't swear just for the hell of it. (He fingers his galluses) You see, I figure language is a poor enough means of communication as it is. So we ought to use all the words we've got. Besides, there are damned few words that everybody understands.

RACHEL

You don't care anything about Bert! You just want a chance to make speeches against the Bible!

DRUMMOND

I care a great deal about Bert. I care a great deal about what Bert thinks.

RACHEL

Well, I care about what the people in this town think of him.

DRUMMOND
(Quietly)

Can you buy back his respectability by making him a coward? (He spades his hands in his hip pockets) I understand what Bert's going through. It's the loneliest feeling in the world—to find yourself standing up when everybody else is sitting down. To have everybody look at you and say,

"What's the matter with him?" I know. I know what it feels like. Walking down an empty street, listening to the sound of your own footsteps. Shutters closed, blinds drawn, doors locked against you. And you aren't sure whether you're walking toward something, or if you're just walking away. (*He takes a deep breath, then turns abruptly*) Cates, I'll change your plea and we'll call off the whole business—on one condition. If you honestly believe you committed a criminal act against the citizens of this state and the minds of their children. If you honestly believe that you're wrong and the law's right. Then the hell with it. I'll pack my grip and go back to Chicago, where it's a cool hundred in the shade.

RACHEL
(*Eagerly*)
Bert knows he's wrong. Don't you, Bert?

DRUMMOND
Don't prompt the witness.

CATES
(*Indecisive*)
What do you think, Mr. Drummond?

DRUMMOND
I'm here. That tells you what I think. (*He looks squarely at* CATES) Well, what's the verdict, Bert? You want to find yourself guilty before the jury does?

CATES
(*Quietly, with determination*)
No, sir. I'm not gonna quit.

RACHEL
(*Protesting*)
Bert!

CATES

It wouldn't do any good now, anyhow. *(He turns to* RACHEL*)* If you'll stick by me, Rache—well, we can fight it out.

(He smiles at her wanly. All the others have gone now, except MEEKER *and* DRUMMOND. RACHEL *shakes her head, bewildered, tears forming in her eyes.)*

RACHEL

I don't know what to do; I don't know what to do.

CATES
(Frowning)

What's the matter, Rache?

RACHEL

I don't want to do it, Bert; but Mr. Brady says—

DRUMMOND

What does Brady say?

RACHEL
(Looking down)

They want me to testify against Bert.

CATES
(Stunned)

You can't!

MEEKER

I don't mean to rush you, Bert; but we gotta close up the shop.

*(CATES *is genuinely panicked.)*

CATES

Rache, some of the things I've talked to you about are things you just say to your own heart. *(He starts to go with* MEEKER, *then turns back)* If you get up on the stand and say those things out loud—*(He shakes his head)* Don't you understand? The words I've said to you—softly, in the dark—just trying to figure out what the stars are for, or what might be on the back side of the moon—

MEEKER
Bert—

CATES
They were questions, Rache. I was just asking questions. If you repeat those things on the witness stand, Brady'll make 'em sound like answers. And they'll crucify me!

(CATES *and* MEEKER *go off. The lights are slowly dimming.* DRUMMOND *puts on his coat, sizing up* RACHEL *as he does so.* RACHEL, *torn, is almost unconscious of his presence or of her surroundings.*)

DRUMMOND
(*Kindly, quietly*)
What's your name? Rachel what?

RACHEL
Rachel Brown. Can they make me testify?

DRUMMOND
I'm afraid so. It would be nice if nobody ever had to *make* anybody do anything. But—(*He takes his brief case*) Don't let Brady scare you. He only *seems* to be bigger than the law.

RACHEL
It's not Mr. Brady. It's my father.

DRUMMOND
Who's your father?

RACHEL
The Reverend Jeremiah Brown. (DRUMMOND *whistles softly through his teeth*) I remember feeling this way when I was a little girl. I would wake up at night, terrified of the dark. I'd think sometimes that my bed was on the ceiling,

and the whole house was upside down; and if I didn't hang onto the mattress, I might fall outward into the stars. *(She shivers a little, remembering)* I wanted to run to my father, and have him tell me I was safe, that everything was all right. But I was always more frightened of him than I was of falling. It's the same way now.

DRUMMOND
(Softly)
Is your mother dead?

RACHEL
I never knew my mother. *(Distraught)* Is it true? *Is* Bert wicked?

DRUMMOND
(With simple conviction)
Bert Cates is a good man. Maybe even a great one. And it takes strength for a woman to love such a man. Especially when he's a pariah in the community.

RACHEL
I'm only confusing Bert. And he's confused enough as it is.

DRUMMOND
The man who has everything figured out is probably a fool. College examinations notwithstanding, it takes a very smart fella to say "I don't know the answer!"
(DRUMMOND puts on his hat, touches the brim of it as a gesture of good-bye and goes slowly off.)

Curtain

ACT TWO

ACT TWO

SCENE I

The courthouse lawn. The same night. The oppressive heat of the day has softened into a pleasant summer evening. Two lampposts spread a glow over the town square, and TWO WORKMEN are assembling the platform for the prayer meeting. One of the WORKMEN glances up at the READ YOUR BIBLE banner.

FIRST WORKMAN
What're we gonna do about this sign?

SECOND WORKMAN
The Devil don't run this town. Leave it up.
> (BRADY *enters, followed by a knot of reporters.* HORNBECK *brings up the rear; he alone is not bothering to take notes. Apparently this informal press conference has been in progress for some time, and* BRADY *is now bringing it to a climax.*)

BRADY
—and I hope that you will tell the readers of your newspapers that here in Hillsboro we are fighting the fight of the Faithful throughout the world!
> (*All write.* BRADY *eyes* HORNBECK, *leaning lazily, not writing.*)

REPORTER
> (*British accent*)
A question, Mr. Brady.

BRADY

Certainly. Where are you from, young man?

REPORTER

London, sir. Reuters News Agency.

BRADY

Excellent. I have many friends in the United Kingdom.

REPORTER

What is your personal opinion of Henry Drummond?

BRADY

I'm glad you asked me that. I want people everywhere to know I bear no personal animosity toward Henry Drummond. There was a time when we were on the same side of the fence. He gave me active support in my campaign of 1908—and I welcomed it. (*Almost impassioned, speaking at writing tempo, so all the reporters can get it down*) But I say that if my own *brother* challenged the faith of millions, as Mr. Drummond is doing, I would oppose him still! (*The* WORKMEN *pound; the townspeople begin to gather*) I think that's all for this evening, gentlemen. (*The reporters scatter.* BRADY *turns to* HORNBECK) Mr. Hornbeck, my clipping service has sent me some of your dispatches.

HORNBECK

How flattering to know I'm being clipped.

BRADY

It grieves me to read reporting that is so—biased.

HORNBECK

I'm no reporter, Colonel. I'm a critic.

BRADY

I hope you will stay for Reverend Brown's prayer meeting. It may bring you some enlightenment.

HORNBECK

It may. I'm here on a press pass, and I don't intend
To miss any part of the show.

(REVEREND BROWN *enters with* MRS. BRADY *on his
arm.* HORNBECK *passes them jauntily, and crosses
downstage.*)

BRADY

Good evening, Reverend. How are you, Mother?

MRS. BRADY

The Reverend Brown was good enough to escort me.

BRADY

Reverend, I'm looking forward to your prayer meeting.

BROWN

You will find our people are fervent in their belief.

(MRS. BRADY *crosses to her husband.*)

MRS. BRADY

I know it's warm, Matt; but these night breezes can be
treacherous. And you know how you perspire.

(*She takes a small kerchief out of her handbag and tucks it
around his neck. He laughs a little.*)

BRADY

Mother is always so worried about my throat.

BROWN

(*Consulting his watch*)

I always like to begin my meetings at the time announced.

BRADY

Most commendable. Proceed, Reverend. After you.

(BROWN *mounts the few steps to the platform.* BRADY
*follows him, loving the feel of the board beneath his feet.
This is the squared circle where he had fought so many
bouts with the English language, and won. The prayer*

meeting is motion picture, radio, and tent-show to these people. To them, the REVEREND BROWN *is a combination Milton Sills and Douglas Fairbanks. He grasps the podium and stares down at them sternly.* BRADY *is benign. He sits with his legs crossed, an arm crooked over one corner of his chair.* BROWN *is milking the expectant pause. Just as he is ready to speak,* DRUMMOND *comes in and stands at the fringe of the crowd.* BROWN *glowers at* DRUMMOND. *The crowd chants.*)

BROWN

Brothers and sisters, I come to you on the Wings of the Word. The Wings of the Word are beating loud in the treetops! The Lord's Word is howling in the Wind, and flashing in the belly of the Cloud!

WOMAN

I hear it!

MAN

I see it, Reverend!

BROWN

And we *believe* the Word!

ALL

We believe!

BROWN

We believe the Glory of the Word!

ALL

Glory, Glory! Amen, amen!
(RACHEL *comes on, but remains at the fringes of the crowd.*)

BROWN

Hearken to the Word! (*He lowers his voice*) The Word tells

us that the World was created in Seven Days. In the beginning, the earth was without form, and void. And the Lord said, "Let there be light!"

VOICES

Ahhhh . . . !

BROWN

And there *was* light! And the Lord saw the Light and the Light saw the Lord, and the Light said, "Am I good, Lord?" And the Lord said, "Thou art good!"

MAN
(Deep-voiced, singing)
And the evening and the morning were the first day!

VOICES

Amen, amen!

BROWN
(Calling out)
The Lord said, "Let there be Firmament!" And even as He spoke, it was so! And the Firmament bowed down before Him and said, "Am I good, Lord?" And the Lord said, "Thou art good!"

MAN
(Singing)
And the evening and the morning were the second day!

VOICES

Amen, amen!

BROWN
On the Third Day brought He forth the Dry Land, and the Grass, and the Fruit Tree! And on the Fourth Day made He the Sun, the Moon, and the Stars—and He pronounced them Good!

VOICES

Amen.

BROWN

On the Fifth Day He peopled the sea with fish. And the air with fowl. And made He great whales. And He blessed them all. But on the morning of the Sixth Day, the Lord rose, and His eye was dark, and a scowl lay across His face. *(Shouts)* Why? Why was the Lord troubled?

ALL

Why? Tell us why! Tell the troubles of the Lord!

BROWN
(Dropping his voice almost to a whisper)

He looked about Him, did the Lord; at all His handiwork, bowed down before Him. And He said, "It is not good, it is not enough, it is not finished. I . . . shall . . . make . . . Me . . . a . . . Man!"
(The crowd bursts out into an orgy of hosannahs and waving arms.)

ALL

Glory! Hosannah! Bless the Lord who created us!

WOMAN
(Shouting out)

Bow down! Bow down before the Lord!

MAN

Are we good, Lord? Tell us! Are we good?

BROWN
(Answering)

The Lord said, "Yea, thou art good! For I have created ye in My Image, after My Likeness! Be fruitful, and multiply, and replenish the Earth, and subdue it!"

MAN
(Deep-voiced, singing)
The Lord made Man master of the Earth . . . !

ALL
Glory, glory! Bless the Lord!

BROWN
(Whipping 'em up)
Do we believe?

ALL
(In chorus)
Yes!

BROWN
Do we believe the Word?

ALL
(Coming back like a whip-crack)
Yes!

BROWN
Do we believe the Truth of the Word?

ALL
Yes!

BROWN
(Pointing a finger toward the jail)
Do we curse the man who denies the Word?

ALL
(Crescendo, each answer mightier than the one before)
Yes!

BROWN
Do we cast out this sinner in our midst?

ALL

Yes!

> (*Each crash of sound from the crowd seems to strike* RACHEL *physically, and shake her.*)

BROWN

Do we call down hellfire on the man who has sinned against the Word?

ALL
> (*Roaring*)

Yes!

BROWN
> (*Deliberately shattering the rhythm, to go into a frenzied prayer, hands clasped together and lifted heavenward*)

O Lord of the Tempest and the Thunder! O Lord of Righteousness and Wrath! We pray that Thou wilt make a sign unto us! Strike down this sinner, as Thou didst Thine enemies of old, in the days of the Pharaohs! (*All lean forward, almost expecting the heavens to open with a thunderbolt.* RACHEL *is white.* BRADY *shifts uncomfortably in his chair; this is pretty strong stuff, even for him*) Let him feel the terror of Thy sword! For all eternity, let his soul writhe in anguish and damnation—

RACHEL

No! (*She rushes to the platform*) No, Father. Don't pray to destroy Bert!

BROWN

Lord, we call down the same curse on those who ask grace for this sinner—though they be blood of my blood, and flesh of my flesh!

BRADY
> (*Rising, grasping* BROWN'S *arm*)

Reverend Brown, I know it is the great zeal of your faith which makes you utter this prayer! But it is possible to be overzealous, to destroy that which you hope to save—so that nothing is left but emptiness. (BROWN *turns*) Remember the wisdom of Solomon in the Book of Proverbs—(*Softly*) "He that troubleth his own house . . . shall inherit the wind." (BRADY *leads* BROWN *to a chair, then turns to the townspeople*) The Bible also tells us that God forgives His children. And we, the Children of God, should forgive each other. (RACHEL *slips off*) My good friends, return to your homes. The blessings of the Lord be with you all. (*Slowly the townspeople move off, singing and humming "Go Tell It on the Mountain."* BRADY *is left alone on stage with* DRUMMOND, *who still watches him impassively.* BRADY *crosses to* DRUMMOND) We were good friends once. I was always glad of your support. What happened between us? There used to be a mutuality of understanding and admiration. Why is it, my old friend, that you have moved so far away from me?

(*A pause. They study each other.*)

DRUMMOND
(Slowly)

All motion is relative. Perhaps it is *you* who have moved away—by standing still.

(*The words have a sharp impact on* BRADY. *For a moment, he stands still, his mouth open, staring at* DRUMMOND. *Then he takes two faltering steps backward, looks at* DRUMMOND *again, then moves off the stage.* DRUMMOND *stands alone. Slowly the lights fade on the silent man. The curtain falls momentarily.*)

Scene II

The courtroom, two days later. It is bright midday, and the trial is in full swing. The JUDGE is on the bench; the jury, lawyers, officials and spectators crowd the courtroom. HOWARD, the thirteen-year-old boy, is on the witness stand. He is wretched in a starched collar and Sunday suit. The weather is as relentlessly hot as before. BRADY is examining the boy, who is a witness for the prosecution.

BRADY

Go on, Howard. Tell them what else Mr. Cates told you in the classroom.

HOWARD

Well, he said at first the earth was too hot for any life. Then it cooled off a mite, and cells and things begun to live.

BRADY

Cells?

HOWARD

Little bugs like, in the water. After that, the little bugs got to be bigger bugs, and sprouted legs and crawled up on the land.

BRADY

How long did this take, according to Mr. Cates?

HOWARD

Couple million years. Maybe longer. Then comes the fishes and the reptiles and the mammals. Man's a mammal.

BRADY

Along with the dogs and the cattle in the field: did he say that?

HOWARD

Yes, sir.

(DRUMMOND *is about to protest against prompting the witness; then he decides it isn't worth the trouble.*)

BRADY

Now, Howard, how did *man* come out of this slimy mess of bugs and serpents, according to your—"Professor"?

HOWARD

Man was sort of evoluted. From the "Old World Monkeys."

(BRADY *slaps his thigh.*)

BRADY

Did you hear that, my friends? "Old World Monkeys"! According to Mr. Cates, you and I aren't even descended from good American monkeys! (*There is laughter*) Howard, listen carefully. In all this talk of bugs and "Evil-ution," of slime and ooze, did Mr. Cates ever make any reference to God?

HOWARD

Not as I remember.

BRADY

Or the miracle He achieved in seven days as described in the beautiful Book of Genesis?

HOWARD

No, sir.

(BRADY *stretches out his arms in an all-embracing gesture.*)

BRADY

Ladies and gentlemen—

DRUMMOND

Objection! I ask that the court remind the learned counsel that this is not a Chautauqua tent. He is supposed to be submitting evidence to a jury. There are no ladies on the jury.

BRADY

Your Honor, I have no intention of making a speech. There is no need. I am sure that everyone on the jury, everyone within the sound of this boy's voice, is moved by his tragic confusion. He has been taught that he wriggled up like an animal from the filth and the muck below! (*Continuing fervently, the spirit is upon him*) I say that these Bible-haters, these "Evil-utionists," are brewers of poison. And the legislature of this sovereign state has had the wisdom to demand that the peddlers of poison—in bottles or in books—clearly label the products they attempt to sell! (*There is applause.* HOWARD *gulps.* BRADY *points at the boy*) I tell you, if this law is not upheld, this boy will become one of a generation, shorn of its faith by the teachings of Godless science! But if the full penalty of the law is meted out to Bertram Cates, the faithful the whole world over, who are watching us here, and listening to our every word, will call this courtroom blessed!

(*Applause. Dramatically,* BRADY *moves to his chair. Condescendingly, he waves to* DRUMMOND.)

BRADY

Your witness, sir.

(BRADY *sits.* DRUMMOND *rises, slouches toward the witness stand.*)

DRUMMOND

Well, I sure am glad Colonel Brady didn't make a speech! (*Nobody laughs. The courtroom seems to resent* DRUMMOND'S *gentle ridicule of the orator. To many, there is an effrontery in* DRUMMOND'S *very voice—folksy and relaxed. It's rather like a harmonica following a symphony concert*)

Howard, I heard you say that the world used to be pretty hot.

HOWARD
That's what Mr. Cates said.

DRUMMOND
You figure it was any hotter then than it is right now?

HOWARD
Guess it musta been. Mr. Cates read it to us from a book.

DRUMMOND
Do you know what book?

HOWARD
I guess that Mr. Darwin thought it up.

DRUMMOND
(Leaning on the arm of the boy's chair)
You figure anything's wrong about that, Howard?

HOWARD
Well, I dunno—

DAVENPORT
(Leaping up, crisply)
Objection, Your Honor. The defense is asking that a thirteen-year-old boy hand down an opinion on a question of morality!

DRUMMOND
(To the JUDGE)
I am trying to establish, Your Honor, that Howard—or Colonel Brady—or Charles Darwin—or anyone in this courtroom—or *you*, sir—has the right to *think*!

JUDGE
Colonel Drummond, the right to think is not on trial here.

DRUMMOND
(Energetically)

With all respect to the bench, I hold that the right to think is very much on trial! It is fearfully in danger in the proceedings of this court!

BRADY
(Rises)

A *man* is on trial!

DRUMMOND

A thinking man! And he is threatened with fine and imprisonment because he chooses to speak what he thinks.

JUDGE

Colonel Drummond, would you please rephrase your question.

DRUMMOND
(To HOWARD)

Let's put it this way, Howard. All this fuss and feathers about Evolution, do you think it hurt you any?

HOWARD

Sir?

DRUMMOND

Did it do you any harm? You still feel reasonably fit? What Mr. Cates told you, did it hurt your baseball game any? Affect your pitching arm?
(He punches HOWARD'S right arm playfully.)

HOWARD

No, sir. I'm a leftie.

DRUMMOND

A southpaw, eh? Still honor your father and mother?

> **HOWARD**

Sure.

> **DRUMMOND**

Haven't murdered anybody since breakfast?

> **DAVENPORT**

Objection.

> **JUDGE**

Objection sustained.
>> (DRUMMOND *shrugs.*)

> **BRADY**

Ask him if his Holy Faith in the scriptures has been shattered—

> **DRUMMOND**

When I need your *valuable* help, Colonel, you may rest assured I shall humbly ask for it. (*Turning*) Howard, do you believe everything Mr. Cates told you?

> **HOWARD**
>> (*Frowning*)

I'm not sure. I gotta think it over.

> **DRUMMOND**

Good for you. Your pa's a farmer, isn't he?

> **HOWARD**

Yes, sir.

> **DRUMMOND**

Got a tractor?

> **HOWARD**

Brand new one.

DRUMMOND

You figure a tractor's sinful, because it isn't mentioned in the Bible?

HOWARD
(*Thinking*)

Don't know.

DRUMMOND

Moses never made a phone call. Suppose that makes the telephone an instrument of the Devil?

HOWARD

I never thought of it that way.

BRADY
(*Rising, booming*)

Neither did anybody else! Your Honor, the defense makes the same old error of all Godless men! They confuse material things with the great spiritual realities of the Revealed Word! (*Turning to* DRUMMOND) Why do you bewilder this child? Does Right have no meaning to you, sir?
(BRADY'S *hands are outstretched, palms upward, pleading.* DRUMMOND *stares at* BRADY *long and thoughtfully.*)

DRUMMOND
(*In a low voice*)

Realizing that I may prejudice the case of my client, I must say that "Right" has no meaning to me whatsoever! (*There is a buzz of reaction in the courtroom*) Truth has meaning—as a direction. But one of the peculiar imbecilities of our time is the grid of morality we have placed on human behavior: so that every act of man must be measured against an arbitrary latitude of right and longitude of wrong—in exact minutes, seconds, and degrees! (*He turns to* HOWARD) Do you have any idea what I'm talking about, Howard?

HOWARD

No, sir.

DRUMMOND

Well, maybe you will. Someday. Thank you, son. That's all.

JUDGE

The witness is excused. (*He raps his gavel, but* HOWARD *remains in the chair, staring goop-eyed at his newly found idol*) We won't need you any more, Howard: you can go back to your pa now. (HOWARD *gets up, and joins the spectators*) Next witness.

DAVENPORT

Will Miss Rachel Brown come forward, please?
> (RACHEL *emerges from among the spectators. She comes forward quickly, as if wanting to get the whole thing over with. She looks at no one.* CATES *watches her with a hopeless expression:* Et tu, Brute. MEEKER *swears her in perfunctorily.*)

BRADY

Miss Brown. You are a teacher at the Hillsboro Consolidated School?

RACHEL
(*Flat*)

Yes.

BRADY

So you have had ample opportunity to know the defendant, Mr. Cates, professionally?

RACHEL

Yes.

BRADY
(*With exaggerated gentleness*)

Is Mr. Cates a member of the spiritual community to which you belong?

DRUMMOND
(Rises)

Objection! I don't understand this chatter about "spiritual communities." If the prosecution wants to know if they go to the same church, why doesn't he ask that?

JUDGE

Uh—objection overruled. (DRUMMOND *slouches, disgruntled.* CATES *stares at* RACHEL *disbelievingly, while her eyes remain on the floor. The exchange between* DRUMMOND *and the* JUDGE *seems to have unnerved her, however*) You will answer the question, please.

RACHEL

I did answer it, didn't I? What was the question?

BRADY

Do you and Mr. Cates attend the same church?

RACHEL

Not any more. Bert dropped out two summers ago.

BRADY

Why?

RACHEL

It was what happened with the little Stebbins boy.

BRADY

Would you tell us about that, please?

RACHEL

The boy was eleven years old, and he went swimming in the river, and got a cramp, and drowned. Bert felt awful about it. He lived right next door, and Tommy Stebbins used to come over to the boarding house and look through Bert's microscope. Bert said the boy had a quick mind, and he might even be a scientist when he grew up. At the fu-

neral, Pa preached that Tommy didn't die in a state of
grace, because his folks had never had him baptized—
> (CATES, *who has been smoldering through this recitation,*
> *suddenly leaps angrily to his feet.*)

CATES

Tell 'em what your father really said! That Tommy's soul
was damned, writhing in hellfire!

DUNLAP
> (*Shaking a fist at* CATES)

Cates, you sinner!
> (*The* JUDGE *raps for order. There is confusion in the*
> *courtroom.*)

CATES

Religion's supposed to comfort people, isn't it? Not
frighten them to death!

JUDGE

We will have order, please!
> (DRUMMOND *tugs* CATES *back to his seat.*)

DRUMMOND

Your Honor, I request that the defendant's remarks be
stricken from the record.
> (*The* JUDGE *nods.*)

BRADY

But how can we strike this young man's bigoted opinions
from the memory of this community? (BRADY *turns, about*
to play his trump card) Now, my dear. Will you tell the
jury some more of Mr. Cates' opinions on the subject of
religion?

DRUMMOND

Objection! Objection! Objection! Hearsay testimony is
not admissible.

JUDGE

The court sees no objection to this line of questioning. Proceed, Colonel Brady.

BRADY

Will you merely repeat in your own words some of the conversations you had with the defendant?

(RACHEL'S *eyes meet* BERT'S. *She hesitates.*)

RACHEL

I don't remember exactly—

BRADY
(*Helpfully*)

What you told me the other day. That presumably "humorous" remark Mr. Cates made about the Heavenly Father.

RACHEL

Bert said—
(*She stops.*)

BRADY

Go ahead, my dear.

RACHEL
(*Pathetically*)

I can't—

JUDGE

May I remind you, Miss Brown, that you are testifying under oath, and it is unlawful to withhold pertinent information.

RACHEL

Bert was just talking about some of the things he'd read. He—He—

BRADY

Were you shocked when he told you these things?
(RACHEL *looks down*) Describe to the court your inner-
most feelings when Bertram Cates said to you: "God did
not create Man! Man created God!"
(*There is a flurry of reaction.*)

DRUMMOND
(*Leaping to his feet*)

Objection!

RACHEL
(*Blurting*)

Bert didn't say that! He was just joking. What he said was:
"God created Man in His own image—and Man, being a
gentleman, returned the compliment."
(HORNBECK *guffaws and pointedly scribbles this down.*
BRADY *is pleased.* RACHEL *seems hopelessly torn.*)

BRADY

Go on, my dear. Tell us some more. What did he say about
the holy state of matrimony? Did he compare it with the
breeding of animals?

RACHEL

No, he didn't say that—He didn't *mean* that. That's not
what I told you. All he said was—
(*She opens her mouth to speak, but nothing comes out. An
emotional block makes her unable to utter a sound. Her
lips move wordlessly.*)

JUDGE

Are you ill, Miss Brown? Would you care for a glass of
water?
(*The fatuity of this suggestion makes* RACHEL *crumble
into a near breakdown.*)

BRADY

Under the circumstances, I believe the witness should be dismissed.

DRUMMOND

And will the defense have no chance to challenge some of these statements the prosecutor has put in the mouth of the witness?

(CATES *is moved by* RACHEL'S *obvious distress.*)

CATES
(*To* DRUMMOND)

Don't plague her. Let her go.

DRUMMOND
(*Pauses, then sighs*)

No questions.

JUDGE

For the time being, the witness is excused. (REVEREND BROWN *comes forward to help his daughter from the stand. His demeanor is unsympathetic as he escorts her from the courtroom. There is a hushed babble of excitement*) Does the prosecution wish to call any further witnesses?

DAVENPORT

Not at the present time, Your Honor.

JUDGE

We shall proceed with the case for the defense. Colonel Drummond.

DRUMMOND
(*Rising*)

Your Honor, I wish to call Dr. Amos D. Keller, head of the Department of Zoology at the University of Chicago.

BRADY

Objection.

(DRUMMOND *turns, startled.*)

DRUMMOND

On what grounds?

BRADY

I wish to inquire what possible relevance the testimony of a Zoo-ology professor can have in this trial.

DRUMMOND
(Reasonably)

It has every relevance! My client is on trial for teaching Evolution. Any testimony relating to his alleged infringement of the law must be admitted!

BRADY

Irrelevant, immaterial, inadmissible.

DRUMMOND
(Sharply)

Why? If Bertram Cates were accused of murder, would it be irrelevant to call expert witnesses to examine the weapon? Would you rule out testimony that the so-called murder weapon was incapable of firing a bullet?

JUDGE

I fail to grasp the learned counsel's meaning.

DRUMMOND

Oh. *(With exaggerated gestures, as if explaining things to a small child)* Your Honor, the defense wishes to place Dr. Keller on the stand to explain to the gentlemen of the jury exactly what the evolutionary theory is. How can they pass judgment on it if they don't know what it's all about?

BRADY

I hold that the very law we are here to enforce excludes such testimony! The people of this state have made it very clear that they do not want this *zoo*-ological hogwash slobbered around the schoolrooms! And I refuse to allow these agnostic scientists to employ this courtroom as a sounding board, as a platform from which they can shout their heresies into the headlines!

JUDGE
(After some thoughtful hesitation)
Colonel Drummond, the court rules that zoology is irrelevant to the case.
(The JUDGE flashes his customary mechanical and humorless grin.)

DRUMMOND
Agnostic scientists! Then I call Dr. Allen Page— *(Staring straight at BRADY)* Deacon of the Congregational Church— and professor of geology and archeology at Oberlin College.

BRADY
(Drily)
Objection!

JUDGE
Objection sustained.
(Again, the meaningless grin.)

DRUMMOND
(Astonished)
In one breath, does the court deny the existence of zoology, geology and archeology?

JUDGE
We do not deny the existence of these sciences: but they do not relate to this point of law.

DRUMMOND
(Fiery)
I call Walter Aaronson, philosopher, anthropologist, au-

thor! One of the most brilliant minds in the world today! Objection, Colonel Brady?

BRADY
(Nodding, smugly)
Objection.

DRUMMOND
Your Honor! The Defense has brought to Hillsboro—at great expense and inconvenience—fifteen noted scientists! The great thinkers of our time! Their testimony is basic to the defense of my client. For it is my intent to show this court that what Bertram Cates spoke quietly one spring afternoon in the Hillsboro High School is no crime! It is incontrovertible as geometry in every enlightened community of minds!

JUDGE
In *this* community, Colonel Drummond—and in this sovereign state—exactly the opposite is the case. The language of the law is clear; we do not need experts to question the validity of a law that is already on the books.
(DRUMMOND, for once in his life has hit a legal roadblock.)

DRUMMOND
(Scowling)
In other words, the court rules out any expert testimony on Charles Darwin's *Origin of Species* or *Descent of Man*?

JUDGE
The court so rules.
(DRUMMOND is flabbergasted. His case is cooked and he knows it. He looks around helplessly.)

DRUMMOND
(There's the glint of an idea in his eye)
Would the court admit expert testimony regarding a book known as the Holy Bible?

JUDGE
(Hesitates, turns to BRADY)
Any objection, Colonel Brady?

BRADY
If the counsel can advance the case of the defendant through the use of the Holy Scriptures, the prosecution will take no exception!

DRUMMOND
Good! *(With relish)* I call to the stand one of the world's foremost experts on the Bible and its teachings—Matthew Harrison Brady!
(There is an uproar in the courtroom. The JUDGE raps for order.)

DAVENPORT
Your Honor, this is preposterous!

JUDGE
(Confused)
I—well, it's highly unorthodox. I've never known an instance where the defense called the prosecuting attorney as a witness.
(BRADY rises. Waits for the crowd's reaction to subside.)

BRADY
Your Honor, this entire trial is unorthodox. If the interests of Right and Justice will be served, I will take the stand.

DAVENPORT
(Helplessly)
But Colonel Brady—
(Buzz of awed reaction. The giants are about to meet head-on. The JUDGE raps the gavel again, nervously.)

JUDGE
(To BRADY)
The court will support you if you wish to decline to testify—as a witness against your own case. . . .

BRADY
(With conviction)

Your Honor, I shall not testify *against* anything. I shall speak out, as I have all my life—on behalf of the Living Truth of the Holy Scriptures!

(DAVENPORT sits, resigned but nervous.)

JUDGE
(To MEEKER, in a nervous whisper)

Uh—Mr. Meeker, you'd better swear in the witness, please . . .

(DRUMMOND moistens his lips in anticipation. BRADY moves to the witness stand in grandiose style. MEEKER holds out a Bible. BRADY puts his left hand on the book, and raises his right hand.)

MEEKER

Do you solemnly swear to tell the truth, the whole truth, and nothing but the truth, so help you God?

BRADY
(Booming)

I do.

MRS. KREBS

And he will!

(BRADY sits, confident and assured. His air is that of a benign and learned mathematician about to be quizzed by a schoolboy on matters of short division.)

DRUMMOND

Am I correct, sir, in calling on you as an authority on the Bible?

BRADY

I believe it is not boastful to say that I have studied the Bible as much as any layman. And I have tried to live according to its precepts.

DRUMMOND

Bully for you. Now, I suppose you can quote me chapter and verse right straight through the King James Version, can't you?

BRADY

There are many portions of the Holy Bible that I have committed to memory.
(DRUMMOND *crosses to counsel table and picks up a copy of Darwin.*)

DRUMMOND

I don't suppose you've memorized many passages from the *Origin of Species?*

BRADY

I am not in the least interested in the pagan hypotheses of that book.

DRUMMOND

Never read it?

BRADY

And I never will.

DRUMMOND

Then how in perdition do you have the gall to whoop up this holy war against something you don't know anything about? How can you be so cocksure that the body of scientific knowledge systematized in the writings of Charles Darwin is, in any way, irreconcilable with the spirit of the Book of Genesis?

BRADY

Would you state that question again, please?

DRUMMOND

Let me put it this way. (*He flips several pages in the book*) On page nineteen of *Origin of Species*, Darwin states—
(DAVENPORT *leaps up.*)

DAVENPORT

I object to this, Your Honor. Colonel Brady has been called as an authority on the Bible. Now the "gentleman from Chicago" is using this opportunity to read into the record scientific testimony which you, Your Honor, have previously ruled is irrelevant. If he's going to examine Colonel Brady on the Bible, let him stick to the Bible, the Holy Bible, and only the Bible!

(DRUMMOND *cocks an eye at the bench.*)

JUDGE
(*Clears his throat*)

You will confine your questions to the Bible.

(DRUMMOND *slaps shut the volume of Darwin.*)

DRUMMOND
(*Not angrily*)

All right. I get the scent in the wind. (*He tosses the volume of Darwin on the counsel table*) We'll play in *your* ball park, Colonel. (*He searches for a copy of the Bible, finally gets* MEEKER'S. *Without opening it,* DRUMMOND *scrutinizes the binding from several angles*) Now let's get this straight. Let's get it clear. This *is* the book that you're an expert on?

(BRADY *is annoyed at* DRUMMOND'S *elementary attitude and condescension.*)

BRADY

That is correct.

DRUMMOND

Now tell me. Do you feel that every word that's written in this book should be taken literally?

BRADY

Everything in the Bible should be accepted, exactly as it is given there.

DRUMMOND
(Leafing through the Bible)

Now take this place where the whale swallows Jonah. Do you figure that actually happened?

BRADY

The Bible does not say "a whale," it says "a big fish."

DRUMMOND

Matter of fact, it says "a great fish"—but it's pretty much the same thing. What's your feeling about that?

BRADY

I believe in a God who can make a whale and who can make a man and make both do what He pleases!

VOICES

Amen, amen!

DRUMMOND
(Turning sharply to the clerk)

I want those "Amens" in the record! *(He wheels back to* BRADY*)* I recollect a story about Joshua, making the sun stand still. Now as an expert, you tell me that's as true as the Jonah business. Right? *(*BRADY *nods, blandly)* That's a pretty neat trick. You suppose Houdini could do it?

BRADY

I do not question or scoff at the miracles of the Lord—as do ye of little faith.

DRUMMOND

Have you ever pondered just what would naturally happen to the earth if the sun stood still?

BRADY

You can testify to that if I get you on the stand.
(There is laughter.)

DRUMMOND

If they say that the sun stood still, they must've had a notion that the sun moves around the earth. Think that's the way of things? Or don't you believe the earth moves around the sun?

BRADY

I have faith in the Bible!

DRUMMOND

You don't have much faith in the solar system.

BRADY
(*Doggedly*)

The sun stopped.

DRUMMOND

Good. (*Level and direct*) Now if what you say factually happened—if Joshua halted the sun in the sky—that means the earth stopped spinning on its axis; continents toppled over each other, mountains flew out into space. And the earth, arrested in its orbit, shriveled to a cinder and crashed into the sun. (*Turning*) How come they missed *this* tidbit of news.

BRADY

They missed it because it didn't happen.

DRUMMOND

It must've happened! According to natural law. Or don't you believe in natural law, Colonel? Would you like to ban Copernicus from the classroom, along with Charles Darwin? Pass a law to wipe out all the scientific development since Joshua. Revelations—period!

BRADY
(*Calmly, as if instructing a child*)

Natural law was born in the mind of the Heavenly Father.

He can change it, cancel it, use it as He pleases. It constantly amazes me that you apostles of science, for all your supposed wisdom, fail to grasp this simple fact.

(DRUMMOND *flips a few pages in the Bible.*)

DRUMMOND

Listen to this: Genesis 4:16. "And Cain went out from the presence of the Lord, and dwelt in the land of Nod, on the East of Eden. And Cain *knew his wife!*" Where the hell did *she* come from?

BRADY

Who?

DRUMMOND

Mrs. Cain. Cain's wife. If, "In the beginning" there were only Adam and Eve, and Cain and Abel, where'd this extra woman spring from? Ever figure that out?

BRADY
(Cool)

No, sir. I will leave the agnostics to hunt for her.
(*Laughter.*)

DRUMMOND

Never bothered you?

BRADY

Never bothered me.

DRUMMOND

Never tried to find out?

BRADY

No.

DRUMMOND

Figure somebody pulled off another creation, over in the next county?

BRADY

The Bible satisfies me, it is enough.

DRUMMOND

It frightens me to imagine the state of learning in this world if everyone had your driving curiosity.
(DRUMMOND *is still probing for a weakness in Goliath's armor. He thumbs a few pages further in the Bible.*)

DRUMMOND

This book now goes into a lot of "begats." (*He reads*) "And Aphraxad begat Salah; and Salah begat Eber" and so on and so on. These pretty important folks?

BRADY

They are the generations of the holy men and women of the Bible.

DRUMMOND

How did they go about all this "begatting"?

BRADY

What do you mean?

DRUMMOND

I mean, did people "begat" in those days about the same way they get themselves "begat" today?

BRADY

The process is about the same. I don't think your scientists have improved it any.
(*Laughter.*)

DRUMMOND

In other words, these folks were conceived and brought forth through the normal biological function known as *sex.* (*There is hush-hush reaction through the court.* HOWARD'S *mother clamps her hands over the boy's ears, but he wriggles free*) What do you think of sex, Colonel Brady?

BRADY

In what spirit is this question asked?

DRUMMOND

I'm not asking what you think of sex as a father, or as a husband. Or a Presidential candidate. You're up here as an expert on the Bible. What's the Biblical evaluation of sex?

BRADY

It is considered "Original Sin."

DRUMMOND
(With mock amazement)

And all these holy people got themselves "begat" through "Original Sin"? (BRADY *does not answer. He scowls, and shifts his weight in his chair*) All this sinning make 'em any less holy?

DAVENPORT

Your Honor, where is this leading us? What does it have to do with the State versus Bertram Cates.

JUDGE

Colonel Drummond, the court must be satisfied that this line of questioning has some bearing on the case.

DRUMMOND
(Fiery)

You've ruled out all my witnesses. I must be allowed to examine the one witness you've left me in my own way!

BRADY
(With dignity)

Your Honor, I am willing to sit here and endure Mr. Drummond's sneering and his disrespect. For he is pleading the case of the prosecution by his contempt for all that is holy.

DRUMMOND

I object, I object, I object.

BRADY

On what grounds? Is it possible that something *is* holy to the celebrated agnostic?

DRUMMOND

Yes! (His voice drops, intensely) The individual human mind. In a child's power to master the multiplication table there is more sanctity than in all your shouted "Amens!", "Holy, Holies!" and "Hosannahs!" An idea is a greater monument than a cathedral. And the advance of man's knowledge is more of a miracle than any sticks turned to snakes, or the parting of waters! But are we now to halt the march of progress because Mr. Brady frightens us with a fable? *(Turning to the jury, reasonably)* Gentlemen, progress has never been a bargain. You've got to pay for it. Sometimes I think there's a man behind a counter who says, "All right, you can have a telephone; but you'll have to give up privacy, the charm of distance. Madam, you may vote; but at a price; you lose the right to retreat behind a powder-puff or a petticoat. Mister, you may conquer the air; but the birds will lose their wonder, and the clouds will smell of gasoline!" *(Thoughtfully, seeming to look beyond the courtroom)* Darwin moved us forward to a hilltop, where we could look back and see the way from which we came. But for this view, this insight, this knowledge, we must abandon our faith in the pleasant poetry of Genesis.

BRADY

We must *not* abandon faith! Faith is the important thing!

DRUMMOND

Then why did God plague us with the power to think? Mr. Brady, why do you deny the *one* faculty which lifts man above all other creatures on the earth: the power of his brain to reason. What other merit have we? The elephant is larger, the horse is stronger and swifter, the butterfly more beautiful, the mosquito more prolific, even the simple sponge is more durable! (*Wheeling on* BRADY) Or does a *sponge* think?

BRADY

I don't know. I'm a man, not a sponge.
(There are a few snickers at this; the crowd seems to be slipping away from BRADY and aligning itself more and more with DRUMMOND.)

DRUMMOND

Do you think a sponge thinks?

BRADY

If the Lord wishes a sponge to think, it thinks.

DRUMMOND

Does a man have the same privileges that a sponge does?

BRADY

Of course.

DRUMMOND

(Roaring, for the first time: stretching his arm toward CATES)
This man wishes to be accorded the same privilege as a sponge! *He wishes to think!*
(There is some applause. The sound of it strikes BRADY *exactly as if he had been slapped in the face.)*

BRADY

But your client is wrong! He is deluded! He has lost his way!

DRUMMOND

It's sad that we aren't all gifted with your positive knowl-edge of Right and Wrong, Mr. Brady. (DRUMMOND *strides to one of the uncalled witnesses seated behind him and takes from him a rock, about the size of a tennis ball.* DRUMMOND *weighs the rock in his hand as he saunters back toward* BRADY) How old do you think this rock is?

BRADY
(Intoning)
I am more interested in the Rock of Ages, than I am in the Age of Rocks.
(A couple of die-hard "Amens." DRUMMOND *ignores this glib gag.)*

DRUMMOND
Dr. Page of Oberlin College tells me that this rock is at least ten million years old.

BRADY
(Sarcastically)
Well, well, Colonel Drummond! You managed to sneak in some of that scientific testimony after all.
(DRUMMOND opens up the rock, which splits into two halves. He shows it to BRADY.)

DRUMMOND
Look, Mr. Brady. These are the fossil remains of a pre-historic marine creature, which was found in this very county—and which lived here millions of years ago, when these very mountain ranges were submerged in water.

BRADY
I know. The Bible gives a fine account of the flood. But your professor is a little mixed up on his dates. That rock is not more than six thousand years old.

DRUMMOND
How do you know?

BRADY
A fine Biblical scholar, Bishop Usher, has determined for

us the exact date and hour of the Creation. It occurred in the year 4004 B.C.

DRUMMOND
That's Bishop Usher's opinion.

BRADY
It is not an opinion. It is literal fact, which the good Bishop arrived at through careful computation of the ages of the prophets as set down in the Old Testament. In fact, he determined that the Lord began the Creation on the 23rd of October in the Year 4004 B.C. at—uh, at 9 A.M.!

DRUMMOND
That Eastern Standard Time? (*Laughter*) Or Rocky Mountain Time? (*More laughter*) It wasn't daylight-saving time, was it? Because the Lord didn't make the sun until the fourth day!

BRADY
(*Fidgeting*)
That is correct.

DRUMMOND
(*Sharply*)
The first day. Was it a twenty-four-hour day?

BRADY
The Bible says it was a day.

DRUMMOND
There wasn't any sun. How do you know how long it was?

BRADY
(*Determined*)
The Bible says it was a day.

DRUMMOND
A normal day, a literal day, a twenty-four-hour day?
(*Pause. BRADY is unsure.*)

BRADY

I do not know.

DRUMMOND

What do you think?

BRADY
(Floundering)

I do not think about things that . . . I do not think about!

DRUMMOND

Do you ever think about things that you *do* think about?
*(There is some laughter. But it is dampened by the knowledge
and awareness throughout the courtroom, that the trap is about
to be sprung)* Isn't it possible that first day was twenty-five
hours long? There was no way to measure it, no way to
tell! *Could* it have been twenty-five hours?
(Pause. The entire courtroom seems to lean forward.)

BRADY
(Hesitates—then)

It is . . . *possible* . . .
*(DRUMMOND'S got him. And he knows it! This is the
turning point. From here on, the tempo mounts. DRUM-
MOND is now fully in the driver's seat. He pounds his
questions faster and faster.)*

DRUMMOND

Oh. You interpret that the first day recorded in the Book
of Genesis could be of indeterminate length.

BRADY
(Wriggling)

I mean to state that the day referred to is not necessarily a
twenty-four-hour day.

DRUMMOND

It could have been thirty hours! Or a month! Or a year!

Or a hundred years! (*He brandishes the rock underneath* BRADY'S *nose*) *Or ten million years!*

(DAVENPORT *is able to restrain himself no longer. He realizes that* DRUMMOND *has* BRADY *in his pocket. Red-faced, he leaps up to protest.*)

DAVENPORT

I protest! This is not only irrelevant, immaterial—it is *illegal!* (*There is excited reaction in the courtroom. The* JUDGE *pounds for order, but the emotional tension will not subside*) I demand to know the purpose of Mr. Drummond's examination! What is he trying to do?

(*Both* BRADY *and* DRUMMOND *crane forward, hurling their answers not at the court, but at each other.*)

BRADY

I'll tell you what he's trying to do! He wants to destroy everybody's belief in the Bible, and in God!

DRUMMOND

You know that's not true. I'm trying to stop you bigots and ignoramuses from controlling the education of the United States! And you know it!

(*Arms out,* DAVENPORT *pleads to the court, but is unheard. The* JUDGE *hammers for order.*)

JUDGE
(*Shouting*)

I shall ask the bailiff to clear the court, unless there is order here.

BRADY

How dare you attack the Bible?

DRUMMOND

The Bible is a book. A good book. But it's not the *only* book.

BRADY

It is the revealed word of the Almighty. God spake to the men who wrote the Bible.

DRUMMOND

And how do you know that God didn't "spake" to Charles Darwin?

BRADY

I know, because God tells me to oppose the evil teachings of that man.

DRUMMOND

Oh. God speaks to you.

BRADY

Yes.

DRUMMOND

He tells you exactly what's right and what's wrong?

BRADY
(Doggedly)

Yes.

DRUMMOND

And you act accordingly?

BRADY

Yes.

DRUMMOND

So you, Matthew Harrison Brady, through oratory, legislation, or whatever, pass along God's orders to the rest of the world! *(Laughter begins)* Gentlemen, meet the "Prophet From Nebraska!"

(BRADY'S *oratory is unassailable; but his vanity—exposed by* DRUMMOND'S *prodding—is only funny. The laughter is painful to* BRADY. *He starts to answer* DRUMMOND, *then turns toward the spectators and tries, almost physically, to suppress the amused reaction. This only makes it worse.)*

BRADY
(*Almost inarticulate*)
I—Please—!

DRUMMOND
(*With increasing tempo, closing in*)
Is that the way of things? God tells Brady what is good! To be against Brady is to be against God!
(*More laughter.*)

BRADY
(*Confused*)
No, no! Each man is a free agent—

DRUMMOND
Then what is Bertram Cates doing in the Hillsboro jail? (*Some applause*) Suppose Mr. Cates had enough influence and lung power to railroad through the State Legislature a law that only *Darwin* should be taught in the schools!

BRADY
Ridiculous, ridiculous! There is only one great Truth in the world—

DRUMMOND
The Gospel according to Brady! God speaks to Brady, and Brady tells the world! Brady, Brady, Brady, Almighty!
(DRUMMOND *bows grandly. The crowd laughs.*)

BRADY
The Lord is my strength—

DRUMMOND
What if a lesser human being—a Cates, or a Darwin—has the audacity to think that God might whisper to *him*? That an un-Brady thought might still be holy? Must men go to prison because they are at odds with the self-appointed prophet? (BRADY *is now trembling so that it is impossible for him to speak. He rises, towering above his*

tormentor—rather like a clumsy, lumbering bear that is baited by an agile dog) Extend the Testaments! Let us have a Book of Brady! We shall hex the Pentateuch, and slip you in neatly between Numbers and Deuteronomy!

(At this, there is another burst of laughter. BRADY *is almost in a frenzy.)*

BRADY
(Reaching for a sympathetic ear, trying to find the loyal audience which has slipped away from him)
My friends—Your Honor—My Followers—Ladies and Gentlemen—

DRUMMOND
The witness is excused.

BRADY
(Unheeding)
All of you know what I stand for! What I believe! I believe, I believe in the truth of the Book of Genesis! *(Beginning to chant)* Exodus, Leviticus, Numbers, Deuteronomy, Joshua, Judges, Ruth, First Samuel, Second Samuel, First Kings, Second Kings—

DRUMMOND
Your Honor, this completes the testimony. The witness is excused!

BRADY
(Pounding the air with his fists)
Isaiah, Jeremiah, Lamentations, Ezekiel, Daniel, Hosea, Joel, Amos, Obadiah—
(There is confusion in the court. The JUDGE *raps.)*

JUDGE
You are excused, Colonel Brady—

BRADY
Jonah, Micah, Nahum, Habakkuk, Zephaniah—

(BRADY *beats his clenched fists in the air with every name.*
There is a rising counterpoint of reaction from the specta-
tors. Gavel.)

JUDGE
(*Over the confusion*)

Court is adjourned until ten o'clock tomorrow morning!
(*Gavel. The spectators begin to mill about. A number of*
them, reporters and curiosity seekers, cluster around DRUM-
MOND. DAVENPORT *follows the* JUDGE *out.*)

DAVENPORT

Your Honor, I want to speak to you about striking all of
this from the record.
(*They go out.*)

BRADY
(*Still erect on the witness stand*)

Haggai, Zechariah, Malachi . . .
(*His voice trails off. He sinks, limp and exhausted into the*
witness chair. MRS. BRADY *looks at her husband, worried*
and distraught. She looks at DRUMMOND *with helpless*
anger. DRUMMOND *moves out of the courtroom, and*
most of the crowd goes with him; Reporters cluster tight
about DRUMMOND, *pads and pencils hard at work.*
BRADY *sits, ignored, on the witness chair.* MEEKER *takes*
CATES *back to the jail.* MRS. BRADY *goes to her husband,*
who still sits on the raised witness chair.)

MRS. BRADY
(*Taking his hand*)

Matt—
(BRADY *looks about to see if everyone has left the court-*
room, before he speaks.)

BRADY

Mother. They're laughing at me, Mother!

MRS. BRADY
(*Unconvincingly*)
No, Matt. No, they're not!

BRADY
I can't stand it when they laugh at me!
(MRS. BRADY *steps up onto the raised level of the witness chair. She stands beside and behind her husband, putting her arms around the massive shoulders and cradling his head against her breast.*)

MRS. BRADY
(*Soothing*)
It's all right, baby. It's all right. (MRS. BRADY *sways gently back and forth, as if rocking her husband to sleep*) Baby . . . Baby . . . !

The curtain falls

ACT THREE

ACT THREE

*The courtroom, the following day. The lighting is low, somber.
A spot burns down on the defense table, where* DRUMMOND
and CATES *sit, waiting for the jury to return.* DRUMMOND
leans back in a meditative mood, feet propped on a chair.
CATES, *the focus of the furor, is resting his head on his arms.
The courtroom is almost empty. Two spectators doze in their
chairs. In comparative shadow,* BRADY *sits, eating a box
lunch. He is drowning his troubles with food, as an alcoholic
escapes from reality with a straight shot.* HORNBECK *enters,
bows low to* BRADY.

HORNBECK
Afternoon, Colonel. Having high tea, I see.
> (BRADY *ignores him*)
Is the jury still out? Swatting flies
And wrestling with justice—in that order?
> (HORNBECK *crosses to* DRUMMOND. CATES *lifts his
> head*)
I'll hate to see the jury filing in;
Won't you, Colonel? I'll miss Hillsboro—
Especially this courthouse:
A melange of Moorish and Methodist;
It must have been designed by a congressman!
> (HORNBECK *smirks at his own joke, then sits in the shad-
> ows and pores over a newspaper. Neither* CATES *nor*
> DRUMMOND *have paid the slightest attention to him.*)

CATES
> (*Staring straight ahead*)
Mr. Drummond. What's going to happen?

DRUMMOND

What do you think is going to happen, Bert?

CATES

Do you think they'll send me to prison?

DRUMMOND

They could.

CATES

They don't ever let you see anybody from the outside, do they? I mean—you can just talk to a visitor—through a window—the way they show it in the movies?

DRUMMOND

Oh, it's not as bad as all that. (*Turning toward the town*) When they started this fire here, they never figured it would light up the whole sky. A lot of people's shoes are getting hot. But you can't be too sure.

(*At the other side of the stage,* BRADY *rises majestically from his debris of paper napkins and banana peels, and goes off.*)

CATES
(*Watching* BRADY *go off*)

He seems so sure. He seems to know what the verdict's going to be.

DRUMMOND

Nobody knows. (*He tugs on one ear*) I've got a pretty good idea. When you've been a lawyer as long as I have—a thousand years more or less—you get so you can smell the way a jury's thinking.

CATES

What are they thinking right now?

DRUMMOND
(*Sighing*)

Someday I'm going to get me an *easy* case. An open-and-shut case. I've got a friend up in Chicago. Big lawyer. Lord how the money rolls in! You know why? He never takes a case unless it's a sure thing. Like a jockey who won't go in a race unless he can ride the favorite.

CATES

You sure picked the long shot this time, Mr. Drummond.

DRUMMOND

Sometimes I think the law *is* like a horse race. Sometimes it seems to me I ride like fury, just to end up back where I started. Might as well be on a merry-go-round, or a rocking horse . . . or . . . (*He half-closes his eyes. His voice is far away, his lips barely move*) Golden Dancer. . . .

CATES

What did you say?

DRUMMOND

That was the name of my first long shot. Golden Dancer. She was in the big side window of the general store in Wakeman, Ohio. I used to stand out in the street and say to myself, "If I had Golden Dancer I'd have everything in the world that I wanted." (*He cocks an eyebrow*) I was seven years old, and a very fine judge of rocking horses. (*He looks off again, into the distance*) Golden Dancer had a bright red mane, blue eyes, and she was gold all over, with purple spots. When the sun hit her stirrups, she was a dazzling sight to see. But she was a week's wages for my father. So Golden Dancer and I always had a plate glass window between us. (*Reaching back for the memory*) But—let's see, it wasn't Christmas; must've been my birthday—I woke up in the morning and there was Golden Dancer at the foot of my bed! Ma had skimped on the groceries, and my father'd worked nights for a month. (*Re-living the moment*) I jumped into the saddle and started to rock— (*Almost a whisper*) And it *broke*! It split in two! The wood was rotten, the whole thing was put together with spit and sealing wax! All shine, and no substance! (*Turning to* CATES) Bert, whenever you see something bright, shining, perfect-seeming—all gold, with purple spots—look behind the paint! And if it's a lie—show it up for what it really is!

(*A* RADIO MAN *comes on, lugging an old-fashioned carbon microphone. The* JUDGE, *carrying his robe over his arm, comes on and scowls at the microphone.*)

RADIO MAN
(*To* JUDGE)

I think this is the best place to put it—if it's all right with you, Your Honor.

JUDGE

There's no precedent for this sort of thing.

RADIO MAN

You understand, sir, we're making history here today. This is the first time a public event has ever been broadcast.

JUDGE

Well, I'll allow it—provided you don't interfere with the business of the court.

(*The* RADIO MAN *starts to string his wires. The* MAYOR *hurries on, worried, brandishing a telegram.*)

MAYOR
(*To* JUDGE)

Merle, gotta talk to you. Over here. (*He draws the* JUDGE *aside, not wanting to be heard*) This wire just came. The boys over at the state capitol are getting worried about how things are going. Newspapers all over are raising such a hullaballoo. After all, November, ain't too far off, and it don't do any of us any good to have any of the voters gettin' all steamed up. Wouldn't do no harm to just let things simmer down. (*The* RADIO MAN *reappears*) Well, go easy, Merle.

(Tipping his hat to DRUMMOND, *the* MAYOR *hurries off.)*

RADIO MAN
(Crisply, into the mike)

Testing. Testing.
    *(*DRUMMOND *crosses to the microphone.)*

DRUMMOND
(To the RADIO MAN*)*

What's that?

RADIO MAN

An enunciator.

DRUMMOND

You going to broadcast?

RADIO MAN

We have a direct wire to WGN, Chicago. As soon as the jury comes in, we'll announce the verdict.
    *(*DRUMMOND *takes a good look at the microphone, fingers the base.)*

DRUMMOND

Radio! God, this is going to break down a lot of walls.

RADIO MAN
(Hastily)

You're—you're not supposed to say "God" on the radio!

DRUMMOND

Why the hell not?
    (The RADIO MAN *looks at the microphone, as if it were a toddler that had just been told the facts of life.)*

RADIO MAN

You're not supposed to say "Hell," either.

DRUMMOND
(Sauntering away)
This is going to be a barren source of amusement!
> *(BRADY re-enters and crosses ponderously to the RADIO MAN.)*

BRADY
Can one speak into either side of this machine?
> *(The RADIO MAN starts at this rumbling thunder, so close to the ear of his delicate child.)*

RADIO MAN
(In an exaggerated whisper)
Yes, sir. Either side.
> *(BRADY attempts to lower his voice, but it is like putting a leash on an elephant.)*

BRADY
Kindly signal me while I am speaking, if my voice does not have sufficient projection for your radio apparatus.
> *(RADIO MAN nods, a little annoyed. HORNBECK smirks, amused. Suddenly the air in the courtroom is charged with excitement. MEEKER hurries on—and the spectators begin to scurry expectantly back into the courtroom. Voices mutter: "They're comin' in now. Verdict's been reached. Jury's comin' back in." MEEKER crosses to the JUDGE'S bench, reaches up for the gavel and raps it several times.)*

MEEKER
Everybody rise. *(The spectators come to attention)* Hear ye, hear ye. Court will reconvene in the case of the State versus Bertram Cates.
> *(MEEKER crosses to lead in the jury. They enter, faces fixed and stern.)*

CATES
(Whispers to DRUMMOND)
What do you think? Can you tell from their faces?

(DRUMMOND *is nervous, too. He squints at the returning jurors, drumming his fingers on the table top.* CATES *looks around, as if hoping to see* RACHEL—*but she is not there. His disappointment is evident. The* RADIO MAN *has received his signal from off-stage, and he begins to speak into the microphone.*)

RADIO MAN
(*Low, with dramatic intensity*)
Ladies and gentlemen, this is Harry Esterbrook, speaking to you from the courthouse in Hillsboro, where the jury is just returning to the courtroom to render its verdict in the famous Hillsboro Monkey Trial case. The Judge has just taken the bench. And in the next few minutes we shall know whether Bertram Cates will be found innocent or guilty.
(*The* JUDGE *looks at him with annoyance. Gingerly, the* RADIO MAN *aims his microphone at the* JUDGE *and steps back. There is hushed tension all through the courtroom.*)

JUDGE
(*Clears his throat*)
Gentlemen of the Jury, have you reached a decision?

SILLERS
(*Rising*)
Yeah. Yes, sir, we have, Your Honor.
(MEEKER *crosses to* SILLERS *and takes a slip of paper from him. Silently, he crosses to the* JUDGE'S *bench again, all eyes following the slip of paper. The* JUDGE *takes it, opens it, raps his gavel.*)

JUDGE
The jury's decision is unanimous. Bertram Cates is found guilty as charged!
(*There is tremendous reaction in the courtroom. Some cheers, applause, "Amens." Some boos.* BRADY *is pleased. But it is not the beaming, powerful, assured* BRADY *of the*

Chautauqua tent. It is a spiteful, bitter victory for him, not a conquest with a cavalcade of angels. CATES *stares at his lap.* DRUMMOND *taps a pencil. The* RADIO MAN *talks rapidly, softly into his microphone. The* JUDGE *does not attempt to control the reaction.)*

HORNBECK
(In the manner of a hawker or pitchman)
Step right up, and get your tickets for the Middle Ages!
You only *thought* you missed the Coronation of Charlemagne!

JUDGE
(Rapping his gavel, shouting over the noise)
Quiet, please! Order! This court is still in session. *(The noise quiets down)* The prisoner will rise, to hear the sentence of this court. *(*DRUMMOND *looks up quizzically, alert)* Bertram Cates, I hereby sentence you to—

DRUMMOND
(Sharply)
Your Honor! A question of procedure!

JUDGE
(Nettled)
Well, sir?

DRUMMOND
Is it not customary in this state to allow the defendant to make a statement before sentence is passed?
(The JUDGE *is red-faced.)*

JUDGE
Colonel Drummond, I regret this omission. In the confusion, and the—I neglected—*(Up, to* CATES) Uh, Mr. Cates, if you wish to make any statement before sentence is passed on you, why, you may proceed.
(Clears throat again. CATES *rises. The courtroom quickly grows silent again.)*

CATES

Your Honor, I am not a public speaker. I do not have the eloquence of some of the people you have heard in the last few days. I'm just a schoolteacher.

MRS. BLAIR

Not any more you ain't!

CATES
(Pause. Quietly)

I *was* a schoolteacher. *(With difficulty)* I feel I am . . . I have been convicted of violating an unjust law. I will continue in the future, as I have in the past, to oppose this law in any way I can. I—

> *(CATES isn't sure exactly what to say next. He hesitates, then sits down. There is a crack of applause. Not from everybody, but from many of the spectators. BRADY is fretful and disturbed. He's won the case. The prize is his, but he can't reach for the candy. In his hour of triumph, BRADY expected to be swept from the courtroom on the shoulders of his exultant followers. But the drama isn't proceeding according to plan. The gavel again. The court quiets down.)*

JUDGE

Bertram Cates, this court has found you guilty of violating Public Act Volume 37, Statute Number 31428, as charged. This violation is punishable by fine and/or imprisonment. *(He coughs)* But since there has been no previous violation of this statute, there is no precedent to guide the bench in passing sentence. *(He flashes the automatic smile)* The court deems it proper—*(He glances at the MAYOR)*—to sentence Bertram Cates to pay a fine of—*(He coughs)* one hundred dollars.

> *(The mighty Evolution Law explodes with the pale puff of a wet firecracker. There is a murmur of surprise through the courtroom. BRADY is indignant. He rises, incredulous.)*

BRADY

Did Your Honor say one hundred dollars?

JUDGE

That is correct. (*Trying to get it over with*) This seems to conclude the business of the trial—

BRADY
(*Thundering*)

Your Honor, the prosecution takes exception! Where the issues are so titanic, the court must mete out more drastic punishment—

DRUMMOND
(*Biting in*)

I object!

BRADY

To make an example of this transgressor! To show the world—

DRUMMOND

Just a minute. Just a minute. The amount of the fine is of no concern to me. Bertram Cates has no intention whatsoever of paying this or any other fine. He would not pay it if it were one single dollar. We will appeal this decision to the Supreme Court of this state. Will the court grant thirty days to prepare our appeal?

JUDGE

Granted. The court fixes bond at . . . five hundred dollars. I believe this concludes the business of this trial. Therefore, I declare this court is adjour—

BRADY
(*Hastily*)

Your Honor! (*He reaches for a thick manuscript*) Your Honor, with the court's permission, I should like to read into the record a few short remarks which I have prepared—

DRUMMOND

I object to that. Mr. Brady may make any remarks he likes—long, short or otherwise. In a Chautauqua tent or in a political campaign. Our business in Hillsboro is completed. The defense holds that the court shall be adjourned.

BRADY
(*Frustrated*)

But I have a few remarks—

JUDGE

And we are all anxious to hear them, sir. But Colonel Drummond's point of procedure is well taken. I am sure that everyone here will wish to remain after the court is adjourned to hear your address. (BRADY *lowers his head slightly, in gracious deference to procedure. The* JUDGE *raps the gavel*) I hereby declare this court is adjourned, sine die.
(*There is a babble of confusion and reaction.* HORNBECK *promptly crosses to* MEEKER *and confers with him in whispers. Spectators, relieved of the court's formality, take a seventh-inning stretch. Fans pump, sticky clothes are plucked away from the skin.*)

MELINDA
(*Calling to* HOWARD, *across the courtroom*)

Which side won?

HOWARD
(*Calling back*)

I ain't sure. But the whole thing's over!
(*A couple of* HAWKERS *slip in the courtroom with Eskimo Pies and buckets of lemonade.*)

HAWKER

Eskimo Pies. Get your Eskimo Pies!
(JUDGE *raps with his gavel.*)

JUDGE
(*Projecting*)

Quiet! Order in the—I mean, your attention, please. (*The spectators quiet down some, but not completely*) We are honored to hear a few words from Colonel Brady, who wishes to address you—

(*The* JUDGE *is interrupted in his introduction by* MEEKER *and* HORNBECK. *They confer sotto voce. The babble of voices crescendos.*)

HAWKER

Get your Eskimo Pies! Cool off with an Eskimo Pie!

(*Spectators flock to get ice cream and lemonade.* BRADY *preens himself for the speech, but is annoyed by the confusion.* HORNBECK *hands the* JUDGE *several bills from his wallet, and* MEEKER *pencils a receipt. The* JUDGE *bangs the gavel again.*)

JUDGE

We beg your attention, please, ladies and gentlemen! Colonel Brady has some remarks to make which I am sure will interest us all!

(*A few of the faithful fall dutifully silent. But the milling about and the slopping of lemonade continues. Two kids chase each other in and out among the spectators, annoying the perspiring* RADIO MAN. BRADY *stretches out his arms, in the great attention-getting gesture.*)

BRADY

My dear friends . . . ! Your attention, please! (*The bugle voice reduces the noise somewhat further. But it is not the eager, anticipatory hush of olden days. Attention is given him, not as the inevitable due of a mighty monarch, but grudgingly and resentfully*) Fellow citizens, and friends of the unseen audience. From the hallowed hills of sacred Sinai, in the days of remote antiquity, came the law which has been our bulwark and our shield. Age upon age, men have looked to the law as they would look to the mountains, whence cometh our strength. And here, here in this—

(The RADIO MAN *approaches* BRADY *nervously.)*

RADIO MAN

Excuse me, Mr.—uh, Colonel Brady; would you . . . uh . . . point more in the direction of the enunciator . . . ?

(The RADIO MAN *pushes* BRADY *bodily toward the microphone. As the orator is maneuvered into position, he seems almost to be an inanimate object, like a huge ornate vase which must be precisely centered on a mantel. In this momentary lull, the audience has slipped away from him again. There's a backwash of restless shifting and murmuring.* BRADY'S *vanity and cussedness won't let him give up, even though he realizes this is a sputtering anticlimax. By God, he'll make them listen!)*

BRADY

(Red-faced, his larynx taut, roaring stridently)

As they would look to the mountains whence cometh our strength. And here, here in this courtroom, we have seen vindicated—*(A few people leave. He watches them desperately, out of the corner of his eye)* We have seen vindicated—

RADIO MAN

(After an off-stage signal)

Ladies and gentlemen, our program director in Chicago advises us that our time here is completed. Harry Y. Esterbrook speaking. We return you now to our studios and "Matinee Musicale."

(He takes the microphone and goes off. This is the final indignity to BRADY; *he realizes that a great portion of his audience has left him as he watches it go.* BRADY *brandishes his speech, as if it were Excalibur. His eyes start from his head, the voice is a tight, frantic rasp.)*

BRADY

From the hallowed hills of sacred Sinai . . .

(He freezes. His lips move, but nothing comes out. Paradoxically, his silence brings silence. The orator can hold his audience only by not speaking.)

STOREKEEPER

Look at him!

MRS. BRADY
(With terror)

Matt—
(There seems to be some violent, volcanic upheaval within him. His lower lip quivers, his eyes stare. Very slowly, he seems to be leaning toward the audience. Then, like a figure in a waxworks, toppling from its pedestal, he falls stiffly, face forward. MEEKER and DAVENPORT spring forward, catch BRADY by the shoulders and break his fall. The sheaf of manuscript, clutched in his raised hand, scatters in mid air. The great words flutter innocuously to the courtroom floor. There is a burst of reaction. MRS. BRADY screams.)

DAVENPORT

Get a doctor!
(Several men lift the prostrate BRADY, and stretch him across three chairs. MRS. BRADY rushes to his side.)

JUDGE

Room! Room! Give him room!

MRS. BRADY

Matt! Dear God in Heaven! Matt!
(DRUMMOND, HORNBECK and CATES watch, silent and concerned—somewhat apart from the crowd. The silence is tense. It is suddenly broken by a fanatic old WOMAN, who shoves her face close to BRADY'S and shrieks.)

WOMAN
(Wailing)

O Lord, work us a miracle and save our Holy Prophet!
(Rudely, MEEKER pushes her back.)

MEEKER
(Contemptuously)
Get away! *(Crisply)* Move him out of here. Fast as we can.
Hank. Bill. Give us a hand here. Get him across the street
to Doc's office.
*(Several men lift BRADY, with difficulty, and begin to
carry him out. A strange thing happens. BRADY begins
to speak in a hollow, distant voice—as if something sealed
up inside of him were finally broken, and the precious con-
tents spilled out into the open at last.)*

BRADY
(As he is carried out; in a strange, unreal voice)
Mr. Chief Justice, Citizens of these United States. During
my term in the White House, I pledge to carry out my program for the betterment of the common people of this
country. As your new President, I say what I have said all
of my life. . . .
*(The crowd tags along, curious and awed. Only DRUM-
MOND, CATES and HORNBECK remain, their eyes fixed
on BRADY'S exit. DRUMMOND stares after him.)*

DRUMMOND
How quickly they can turn. And how painful it can be
when you don't expect it. *(He turns)* I wonder how it feels
to be Almost-President three times—with a skull full of
undelivered inauguration speeches.

HORNBECK
Something happens to an Also-Ran.
Something happens to the feet of a man
Who always comes in second in a foot-race.
He becomes a national unloved child,
A balding orphan, an aging adolescent
Who never got the biggest piece of candy.
Unloved children, of all ages, insinuate themselves
Into spotlights and rotogravures.
They stand on their hands and wiggle their feet.
Split pulpits with their pounding! And their tonsils

Turn to organ pipes. Show me a shouter,
And I'll show you an also-ran. A might-have-been,
An almost-was.

CATES
(Softly)

Did you see his face? He looked terrible. . . .
> (MEEKER *enters.* CATES *turns to him.* MEEKER *shakes his head: "I don't know."*)

MEEKER

I'm surprised more folks ain't keeled over in this heat.

HORNBECK

He's all right. Give him an hour or so
To sweat away the pickles and the pumpernickel.
To let his tongue forget the acid taste
Of vinegar victory.
Mount Brady will erupt again by nightfall,
Spouting lukewarm fire and irrelevant ashes.
> (CATES *shakes his head, bewildered.* DRUMMOND *watches him, concerned.*)

DRUMMOND

What's the matter, boy?

CATES

I'm not sure. Did I win or did I lose?

DRUMMOND

You won.

CATES

But the jury found me—

DRUMMOND

What jury? Twelve men? Millions of people will say you won. They'll read in their papers tonight that you smashed a bad law. You made it a joke!

CATES

Yeah. But what's going to happen now? I haven't got a job.
I'll bet they won't even let me back in the boarding house.

DRUMMOND

Sure, it's gonna be tough, it's not gonna be any church so-
cial for a while. But you'll live. And while they're making
you sweat, remember—you've helped the next fella.

CATES

What do you mean?

DRUMMOND

You don't suppose this kind of thing is ever finished, do
you? Tomorrow it'll be something else—and another fella
will have to stand up. And you've helped give him the
guts to do it!

CATES

(*Turning to* MEEKER, *with new pride in what he's done*)
Mr. Meeker, don't you have to lock me up?

MEEKER

They fixed bail.

CATES

You don't expect a schoolteacher to have five hundred
dollars.

MEEKER

(*Jerking his head toward* HORNBECK)
This fella here put up the money.

HORNBECK

With a year's subscription to the Baltimore *Herald*,
We give away—at no cost or obligation—
A year of freedom.

(RACHEL *enters, carrying a suitcase. She is smiling, and there is a new lift to her head.* CATES *turns and sees her.*)

CATES

Rachel!

RACHEL

Hello, Bert.

CATES

Where are you going?

RACHEL

I'm not sure. But I'm leaving my father.

CATES

Rache . . .

RACHEL

Bert, it's my fault the jury found you guilty. (*He starts to protest*) Partly my fault. I helped. (RACHEL *hands* BERT *a book*) This is your book, Bert. (*Silently, he takes it*) I've read it. All the way through. I don't understand it. What I do understand, I don't like. I don't want to think that men come from apes and monkeys. But I think that's beside the point.

(DRUMMOND *looks at the girl admiringly.*)

DRUMMOND

That's right. That's beside the point.

(RACHEL *crosses to* DRUMMOND.)

RACHEL

Mr. Drummond, I hope I haven't said anything to offend you. You see, I haven't really thought very much. I was always afraid of what I might think—so it seemed safer not to think at all. But now I know. A thought is like a child inside our body. It has to be born. If it dies inside you, part of you dies, too! (*Pointing to the book*) Maybe what Mr. Darwin wrote is bad. I don't know. Bad or good, it doesn't make any difference. The ideas have to come out—like children. Some of 'em healthy as a bean plant, some sickly. I think the sickly ideas die mostly, don't you, Bert?

(BERT *nods yes, but he's too lost in new admiration for her to do anything but stare. He does not move to her side.* DRUMMOND *smiles, as if to say:* "That's quite a girl!" *The* JUDGE *walks in slowly.*)

JUDGE

Brady's dead.

(*They all react. The* JUDGE *starts toward his chambers.*)

DRUMMOND

I can't imagine the world without Matthew Harrison Brady.

CATES

(*To the* JUDGE)

What caused it? Did they say?

(*Dazed, the* JUDGE *goes off without answering.*)

HORNBECK

Matthew Harrison Brady died of a busted belly.

(DRUMMOND *slams down his brief case*)

You know what I thought of him,

And I know what you thought.

Let us leave the lamentations to the illiterate!

Why should we weep for him? He cried enough for himself!

The national tear-duct from Weeping Water, Nebraska,

Who flooded the whole nation like a one-man Mississippi!

You know what he was:

A Barnum-bunkum Bible-beating bastard!

(DRUMMOND *rises, fiercely angry.*)

DRUMMOND

You smart-aleck! You have no more right to spit on his religion than you have a right to spit on *my* religion! Or my lack of it!

HORNBECK
(*Askance*)

Well, what do you know!
Henry Drummond for the defense
Even of his enemies!

DRUMMOND
(*Low, moved*)

There was much greatness in this man.

HORNBECK

Shall I put that in the obituary?
(DRUMMOND *starts to pack up his brief case.*)

DRUMMOND

Write anything you damn please.

HORNBECK

How do you write an obituary
For a man who's been dead thirty years?
"In Memoriam—M.H.B." Then what?
Hail the apostle whose letters to the Corinthians
Were lost in the mail?
Two years, ten years—and tourists will ask the guide,
"Who died here? Matthew Harrison Who?"
(*A sudden thought*)
What did he say to the minister? It fits!
He delivered his own obituary!
(*He looks about the witness stand and the* JUDGE's
bench, searching for something)
They must have one here some place.
(HORNBECK *pounces on a Bible*)
Here it is: *his* book!
(*Thumbing hastily*)
Proverbs, wasn't it?

DRUMMOND
(*Quietly*)

"He that troubleth his own house shall inherit the wind:
and the fool shall be servant to the wise in heart."

(HORNBECK *looks at* DRUMMOND, *surprised. He snaps the Bible shut, and lays it on the* JUDGE'S *bench.* HORNBECK *folds his arms and crosses slowly toward* DRUMMOND, *his eyes narrowing.*)

HORNBECK

We're growing an odd crop of agnostics this year!
(DRUMMOND'S *patience is wearing thin.*)

DRUMMOND
(*Evenly*)

I'm getting damned tired of you, Hornbeck.

HORNBECK

Why?

DRUMMOND

You never pushed a noun against a verb except to blow up something.

HORNBECK

That's a typical lawyer's trick: accusing the accuser!

DRUMMOND

What am I accused of?

HORNBECK

I charge you with contempt of conscience!
Self-perjury. Kindness aforethought.
Sentimentality in the first degree.

DRUMMOND

Why? Because I refuse to erase a man's lifetime? I tell you Brady had the same right as Cates: the right to be wrong!

HORNBECK

"Be-Kind-To-Bigots" Week. Since Brady's dead,
We must be kind. God, how the world is rotten
With kindness!

DRUMMOND

A giant once lived in that body. *(Quietly)* But Matt Brady got lost. Because he was looking for God too high up and too far away.

HORNBECK

You hypocrite! You fraud!
(With a growing sense of discovery)
You're more religious than *he* was!
(DRUMMOND doesn't answer. HORNBECK crosses toward the exit hurriedly)
Excuse me, gentlemen. I must get me to a typewriter
And hammer out the story of an atheist
Who believes in God.
(He goes off.)

CATES

Colonel Drummond.

DRUMMOND

Bert, I am resigning my commission in the State Militia. I hand in my sword!

CATES

Doesn't it cost a lot of money for an appeal? I couldn't pay you . . .
(DRUMMOND waves him off.)

DRUMMOND

I didn't come here to be paid. *(He turns)* Well, I'd better get myself on a train.

RACHEL

There's one out at five-thirteen. Bert, you and I can be on that train, too!

CATES
(Smiling, happy)

I'll get my stuff!

RACHEL

I'll help you!
>*(They start off. RACHEL comes back for her suitcase.*
>*CATES grabs his suit jacket, clasps DRUMMOND'S arm.)*

CATES
>*(Calling over his shoulder)*

See you at the depot!
>*(RACHEL and CATES go off. DRUMMOND is left alone*
>*on stage. Suddenly he notices RACHEL'S copy of Darwin*
>*on the table.)*

DRUMMOND
>*(Calling)*

Say—you forgot—
>*(But RACHEL and CATES are out of earshot. He weighs the*
>*volume in his hand; this one book has been the center of*
>*the whirlwind. Then DRUMMOND notices the Bible, on the*
>*JUDGE'S bench. He picks up the Bible in his other hand; he*
>*looks from one volume to the other, balancing them thought-*
>*fully, as if his hands were scales. He half-smiles, half-shrugs.*
>*Then DRUMMOND slaps the two books together and jams*
>*them in his brief case, side by side. Slowly, he climbs to the*
>*street level and crosses the empty square.)*

The curtain falls